No More Chains Holding Me

*How embracing a re[...]
will unleash freedom in [...]*

FRANCINE DENT, PH.D.

"The Spirit of the Lord God is upon me, Because the Lord has anointed me to bring good news to the afflicted; He has sent me to bind up the brokenhearted, to proclaim liberty to captives and freedom to prisoners; to proclaim the favorable year of the Lord." Isaiah 61: 1

Order this book online at www.trafford.com
or email orders@trafford.com

Most Trafford titles are also available at major online book retailers.

Printed in the United States of America.

ISBN: 978-1-4269-5631-7 (sc)
ISBN: 978-1-4269-5632-4 (hc)
ISBN: 978-1-4269-5659-1 (e)

Library of Congress Control Number: 2011901032

Trafford rev. 03/18/2011

Trafford
PUBLISHING®   www.trafford.com

North America & International
toll-free: 1 888 232 4444 (USA & Canada)
phone: 250 383 6864 ♦ fax: 812 355 4082

ACKNOWLEDGEMENTS

First, I thank God, the head of my life, my Lord and Savior. I thank him for the vision and the ability to write this book. I thank him for each and every one of your breakthroughs and blessings you receive, that come by way of this book.

To Dent, my husband, my partner for life, my friend, and my encourager to keep on writing; you are the flame in my fire, the one who loves me with all of your being and I love you with the same love and compassion. Thank you for all your input, from the man's perspective.

To Bishop Franklin Blanks and Overseer Dr. Stephanie Blanks, nine years ago you asked me to write my short- and long-term goals of which there were seven. You held and are still holding me accountable for each one. This book was the sixth goal completed. Praise God!!!! Thank you for your love, support and for being there whenever I need you.

To my Mom, Dorothy Thornley; my children, Pastors Calvert & Ra'chel Edison, Eric and Shawn Marrow, and Patrick & Sheree Jamieson; to all ten grandchildren and one great grand, you are the ones who help me be the woman I am today, thanks.

To the New Birth Deliverance Ministries family, thank you for your prays, support and love.

To Pastor Rodney, for providing the worship music as a part of the book.

And special thanks to those who read:

L. Alphonso Dent

~ Shawn Marrow ~ Dr. Karyn C. Jones ~ Danae McCain

and edited the book:

Olivia Willis ~ Tiffiney Langston ~ Charlene Stewart

INTRODUCTION

Ten years ago the Lord began to really deal with me concerning the separation and divorce process with my first husband. In doing so, I heard God say, "You are not alone," but that wasn't anything new; during my twenty years of counseling I had heard the same stories. However, this time God's voice was different. I've learned that when God's voice changes it's usually because the directions for our lives are about to change. What was different? It is now my time to write the stories so there will be "No more chains holding you."

We struggle in relationships but we stay, we are hurt but we stay, we war for them and stay, and they almost kill us and we stay. We are emotionally, spiritually, physically and verbally abused and we continue to stay. It's time to say "no more" and find a way out. No more chains have to hold you in captivity.

God showed me how to help you by writing this book. It is an easy read with worksheets, prayers and a worship CD, to assist you in getting free

Along with my own painful story I have intertwined stories of others who were also bound.

It is my prayer that as you read this book, you will hear your own story, open your heart and allow God to release, heal, restore, and free you from the chains that hold you in captivity. Today you can be free! Don't just make the plan but work the plan that has been set before you. Be pressed with the rest to be blessed by the best.

TABLE OF CONTENTS

CHAPTER 1

THE CHILDHOOD BONDAGES

Who are we and what have we become? Is who we are predicated upon our childhood background, culture, environment, and life experiences? Are these experiences the ones that mold, shape and release us into our destinies, or have they bound us in the chains of the very things that were suppose to develop us into positive and productive individuals?

As a country girl growing up in Virginia during the 60-70's, we had a hard but simple life. Country life wasn't a picnic and there was never an end when it came to work and/or chores. Everyone rose early to pick either cotton or tobacco before and after school. You had three sets of clothes: work/play, school and church. Chores had to be completed before and after school; feeding the chickens, gathering eggs, feeding pigs, milking cows or other forms of outside work regardless of the weather. Going to school and back required walking long miles to a one or two room school that was heated for many years with a potbelly stove. There was no such thing as "I'm not going to school," because there were always too many eyes and ears who would discipline any child that got out of line. In addition, going to school was considered as getting a break from having to do chores. If you were bold enough to skip school, whoever caught you would punish you and send you home. They would call your parent or guardian and upon arriving home you were punished again.

In the South days were long and nights were short. You said yes/no mam or sir. As children we knew our place and didn't deviate far from it. After doing homework and completing chores we enjoyed an uncomplicated life, probably because you were too tired to do anything else. On Sunday's when all the family would gather, the girls often played with doll babies, paper dolls, jump rope and hop scotch. Our doll babies and paper dolls permitted us to embrace the challenges of exploring the fantasies of our young lives. No matter what our daily challenges brought we always had time to fantasize about living in big houses with lots of bedrooms, a large kitchen and bathrooms with running water like the ones our parents often worked in; cleaning, cooking, ironing or caring for the boss man's children. It would be accessorized with everything nice that the Sears catalog had to offer. And of course *"they" (the ones we worked for)* would be cleaning and doing for us. Our husbands would look and dress like the ones in the Sears catalog, light complexion, fine hair and coal black eyes.

We had no knowledge of what a professional man was but we wanted him. Forget the hard working, honest family man who did what was necessary for their family to survive. Some of us never knew what struggles they had, what sacrifices were made just so their children could go off to college and have a better life. We wanted what *"they"* said we would never have. We weren't allowed to play with *"their"* kids, eat at *"their"* table or *"their"* eating establishments. But we were ripe for the master's pickings; our mothers or young virgin daughters were good enough for the men to lay with because *"their"* dignified "Lady of the house" didn't want to be disfigured or bothered with pregnancy. To this day we still want what we can't have.

We have been overworked, raped, beaten, and stripped of our dignity, and it continues to happen and yet we continue to open our heart to the same bondages. We are stripped of our identity over and over and afterwards we ask who am I? What is my purpose? When we can't find the answers instead of continuing the search or trying something different, too many of us stay in our painful situations because it's all we know. Venture into the path of the unknown even when directed by God can be so overwhelming that fear grips and paralyzes us. Instead of making necessary changes in our lives we repeat the same behaviors, hang with the same type of people, and fall in the same traps and pitfalls. The vicious cycle doesn't stop but continues with a greater intensity.

We dream, fantasize, and hope for a better life and many of us, to our bewilderment, marry men who are opposite of what we wanted. We even choose men like our fathers who we hated all our lives: strong but irresponsible, the life of the party but overbearing and controlling. Others marry men whom they idealized only to find out that under the green grass on the other side of the fence were infiltrated with snakes. The pretty boy became the womanizer, keeping us with babies while he went out and entertained other fine long haired babes. Because of our insecurities we have allowed this behavior to continue. The snake's job is to destroy our line of defense through lies and deception. We are told by him no one wants us but him and we couldn't make it without him. These lies that we are told keep us locked in and locked down with low self esteem, guilt, despair and depression. Many of us have come from good, responsible, God-ordained families and it was great growing up, but as soon as we get to the age where we think we know more than our parents the snakes come out. We begin looking for a bad boy so we can experience all the things that we thought were missing. Most of us strayed away to alcohol, drugs and more men to fill the void that only God can fill. Many kept going and got in too deep and were tricked into thinking they couldn't turn back. However, some of us returned because the God that's in us just wouldn't allow us to go but so far, thank God.

The lifestyle of girls who grew up in the city was different. The majority of the families were and still are, single parent homes. There were a few fathers who worked hard, came home and supported their families. Others sat on the corner drinking and gambling. Oh the tangled web we weave.

Not having enough money, work or the means to survive on their own, women too often took the abuse of men to keep a roof over their head and food on the table. A good beating they thought was what was necessary to keep a woman in line; when the house wasn't clean enough or the kids were making too much noise, and the list goes on. Before the daughters could begin the development process the dirty men would start fondling and eventually rape the young innocent girls that they were supposed to be caring for. Moms too often turn a deaf ear and a blind eye to things that go on behind closed doors; desperately waiting to hear those three little powerful words "I love You," even when it's all a lie but it feels good. She will sell her children, her values and even her soul. What a great cost to pay for something that has to come from within oneself.

Regardless of your location the role of a woman was to be one who worked in the kitchen, cared for the children and the men, went to church and didn't talk back. A few men and women went to college but they were among the elite. Women weren't allowed to be in the presence of men, old and young, when they were talking or having fun. They had a saying, woman should stay out of men's conversation and children ought to be seen and not heard. The men handled the entire financial obligation leaving most women dependent upon their husbands or fathers for stability and financial freedom.

By the time the city boys reached their teens, many were involved in some street gang, skipping school, running numbers and women or smoking weed. The boys in the city as a whole had no fatherly representation for role models and many young men grew up and repeated the lifestyle that they knew. Their strategy was to see how many girls they could play, have girls fall in love with them, get them pregnant, and leave them to raise their child alone. They blame the girl for being stupid for not protecting herself. Some even boast about how many bastard children they have all the while moving on to the next girl he could run his Mack Daddy lines on.

He sequentially needs to break the bondage of lack of identity, rejection, abandonment, poverty, drugs, and crime. Subsequently, men have feelings just like women and their hurts are just as deep. The difference is they have been taught to hide their feeling because it's a sign of weakness. Therefore boys, young men and older men mask their tears, shame, pain, failures, and all other hurtful situations. They mask behind words like "whatever, it doesn't bother me, I'm tough, I'm a man, so what if you walk out of my life there's other fish in the sea." Instead of dealing with the hurt they become angry, bitter, and vengeful men. One hurt suppressing the next causing generations of angry men. Going against the "good old boys" rule keeps a good man from opening up and talking about what, who and why they are hurting. These men turning these feelings inward cause the lost of self worth, self esteem, value, and most of all, purpose. This is also the number one reason so many young men are living on the street and being disconnected from his family.

Study indicates that very young boys during the early developmental stage without a father or positive role model to guide, protect and show them how to be a real man often leads to emotional, social, spiritual and economical breakdowns; feelings of being unwanted, unloved, rejection and abandonment; alcohol and drug use. These dysfunctions have caused many boys and men to lose their heritage resulting in the loss of purpose that distinguish who they are as an individual. God created man to impart wisdom, love, compassion, faith, mercy and grace into every extension of himself. Therefore men, you too have to break every yoke and bondage and go back to the basic God given abilities that were designed for you since conception. Don't allow another negative influence into your life. Use the same energy that fuels the negative response and command positive changes in your life. Step out of the mess and step into your heritage, your purpose, the real you that you can become.

The upper middle class, the rich and the famous sent their children to boarding school so they didn't have to be bothered with the struggles of parenting. They were more interested in the society lifestyle and making money than spending family time. They often married in that class at the cost of losing their heritage to avoid poverty, shame and disgrace. Both groups of young adults end up with a great void in their lives. Too many of these young people who are running our government, businesses, churches, and homes today are the third and fourth generation of unresolved issues. When rejection, abandonment, identity and esteem issues have not been dealt with as a youth, the struggle to find purpose and balance can be like walking into a web. You know it's there; you can feel it all over you but you don't see it. The more you attempt to get free the more it continues to hold you. If you recall seeing insects that get caught in a web most will die from entrapment or die trying to get out. The learned behavior or a better term the "generational curse" continues. Will someone please take a stand one family at a time and make a difference and break the chain? If one person breaks the chain, we can break the link and if we break the link we can stop the process and start a new generation of hope in a family.

During the 60's and 70's, Sunday's were our only day off from work and a time to relax and have fun. Going to church was considered social freedom. Christians would travel for miles to enjoy the fellowship and be empowered through the Word of God. Many enjoyed being servants of God because a servant was who they were. They worked hard and served God with the same sincerity. Church wasn't a place to dump their pain when this was the only day to rest and unwind. Therefore their pain was masked and never dealt with. There were many secrets in the house and in the church house that kept many females bound. The Word of God kept them in their homes and in their marriages as good wives and mothers. However there is always one or two churches that will use God's word to keep them in check with rules and regulations. As a result, churches stopped being a place of healing and became a place that bound them in religious laws. So not only were they racially and economically bound, but religiously bound as well.

These churches are called cults and are used to trap one in their own faith rather than releasing them to serve God to the fullest of his Glory and power. Crossing those lines would mean that they began to speak their minds, rely on the word that God spoke to them directly without the third party. Trusting and embracing a relationship with the Lord not only brought about healing but deliverance. It is God who made us and not man who controlled us. This Godly liberation angered some men, caused exclusion from ones' faith, and according to them loss of salvation.

Divorce was something that just wasn't publicly heard of until the early 80's with the Women's Liberation Movement. There were new laws introduced that protected women giving us the right and opportunity to speak up and out. Prior to this if a woman was emotionally, spiritually, physically or sexually abused she had little to no recourse. Across the continent there were no racial differences when it came to the cares of a man's woman. Women were treated as men's property. What went on in his house was his business and the police, if any, never got involved except to insure that woman stayed in her place. If a husband beat his wife it was because she needed it; if he chose to have another woman or his daughters it was because she wasn't enough for him or she just couldn't please him.

Some things haven't changed, we still want men that look good, dress good, ride in nice automobiles and live plush and lavish lifestyles. The more bling-bling one has the more we want them without examining the contents of the package. Many men today continue to seek women to cook, clean, care for the children and them; go to work and church; don't talk back, and don't rock the boat.

An article written in Crosswalk stated *"I have seen too many women who are in love with the idea of marriage, who have been planning their weddings since they were little girls and who end up getting married just for the sake of being married. As more and more girls* are raised not to think that marriage in the abstract is an important life goal that they must achieve in order to be considered worthwhile, complete human beings, the longer women will wait to get married and the more they will ensure that the person they are marrying is someone they really want to be with. And, of course, there will also be many more women who will opt out of marriage altogether. And the more boys* are raised* *to consider the opposite sex their true equals, the healthier people's relationships will be. All of that will result in a lower divorce rate, so we'll end up with some steady state number of marriages that just don't work out.*[1]

---

[1] http://pandagon.net/2006/10/05/the-natural-divorce-rate/"\1"comment-209082#comment-209082"\0"Premanent Link to this Comment" http://**ragingred.blogspot.com** Oct 5th, 2006 at 12:40 pm

CHAPTER 2

THE FAMILY

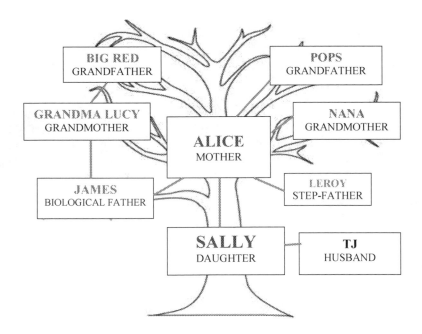

THE FAMILY

There was a little girl name Sally who grew up in an environment of physical and emotional abuse. Alice, her mom was caught between two men; James who was Sally's father, her first love and the love of her life, and Leroy who Alice married some years later.

SALLY'S MOM

Alice grew up in a very loving Christian home. Her parents were Pops and Nana, as they were called by many because they were parents to all who came in contact with them. Pops was the pastor of the community church, therefore, when the church doors were open Alice was right there in church. Church was great but once Alice became a teen she wanted to get involved in school activities but there wasn't any time, and according to Pops those activities were worldly and would only get nice young girls in trouble.

ALICE'S PARENTS

Alice wasn't like her father; she wanted to have some fun, only to find out that the grass wasn't always greener on the other side. Her parents had the best loving relationship she had ever seen. She remembered making a promise as a child that she would choose a good man like Pops, as long as he wasn't a Pastor.

He and Nana would read the bible, study and pray every night for hours before going to bed. Alice asked Nana how she always remained calm even through the heartaches and tragedies people drop on her. She said, "You just have to pray, put all things in God's hand and He will work everything out." We had to sit at the dinner table for hours talking and praying until we knew we had made the right decision. Nana said, "When the three of us; the Lord who is the head of our lives, Pops and I, take out time to talk everything through we never have disagreements over any of our decisions. We have always stayed on God's path even when we didn't understand, knowing we would understand it by and by." Alice thought to herself, surely no one had that much faith. Like Nana knew what she was thinking, she would add, "If God can't fix it then it can't be fixed," and she would leave the room singing "Amazing Grace how sweet the sound that saved a wretch like me," or "His Eye is on the Sparrow and I know He's watching over me." Alice said, that's too much God, but her mother would tell her, "Someday you will learn that God has a perfect plan for your life and if you trust him and obey him you will have peace that will surpass your understanding, and that kind of peace you will not find in the things of the world." Then she said something I wished I had understood then, "Enjoy serving God and it will keep you from looking in all the wrong places."

SALLY'S BIOLOGICALLY FAMILY

James, her biological father, rejected Alice when she was pregnant with Sally. Alice wasn't the right color or good enough to marry into James' family. His father, Big Red was physically abusive and not one to cross. Grandma Lucy, James's mother, was a quiet and gentle woman who knew her place. In her own way Grandma Lucy quietly kept the peace even if it required sending the male children off to the military or away from home to start their own lives. Grandma Lucy hated it when the boys would argue and fight with Big Red to protect her from him when he had been drinking. Otherwise, he was just simply mean and nasty.

Big Red wasn't the one to have on your bad side. If you mess with him he made it his business to get you back in the worst way, even if you were family. Big Red was a notorious numbers runner or bookie in the town. If you owed him money you had to pay it back with interest and if you were one hour late the interest went up 10% per minute. If he had to send someone to find you he would break your hand, leg, or beat you until you wished you were never born.

SALLY'S STEP-FATHER

Leroy was a hard working, overbearing, possessive, jealous, socially functional alcoholic (he drank from the time he left work to the next morning's first sip), who in his own way loved his family. Most of the men in his family carried the same personality defect and behavior. Alice was a hard working loving and giving mother who took too much for the sake of her child. But was it better to take the pain of not being enough woman for him and all the abuse that went with it, over being hurt and abandoned again? Could she keep from going back to that deep dark place where she once was and promised never to go again?

SALLY'S HUSBAND

Sally married TJ, a hard working, womanizing man just like Leroy, her stepfather.

CHAPTER 3

SECRETS

In every family there are secrets; some good, some bad, some that need to come out and others that are detrimental if they are uncovered. Sally's family was no different, there were many secrets that were just as painful going into hiding as coming out. So let's start at the beginning with Alice and see where her life took a detrimental turn.

Alice was a nice young Christian girl. All her life she obeyed her parents and stayed in church. She was a leader of the youth group, teen bible study and a devoted choir member. They lived at the top of the mountain in the middle of nowhere, no neighbors, relatives or friends to play with for miles.

The kids at school knew she was a PK kid (preacher's kid), and living in a small town no one messed with the PK's. Therefore, you weren't liked by many because you received special treatment. But she couldn't understand because she wasn't allowed to do any of the things the other kids could do. They thought she was strange and they often called her ugly. No matter what they tried her braids never laid down. She also had to wear corrective shoes with a leg brace.

By the time she reached the junior year in High School she stopped wearing rejection well and hated having to go school. No one noticed that more and more her self-esteem lowered; she began to withdraw and hide out in her room.

She only had two girls she could call friends. These girls belonged to the same church and they went all the way through school together and were often called the three ugly ducklings. They were all unique in their own way and extremely smart. They stuck together. The oldest of the group was very dark skinned, tall and thin with sandy hair; the youngest girl was short, heavy and spoke with a deep Southern dialect.

During the last months of Alice's senior year of school she decided to come out of her room and have some fun in exchange for serving God. This was her first wrong turn.

One day out of the blue, she met her first boyfriend, James. She was so happy. All the feelings of rejection, low self-esteem, and low self worth she felt were suppressed. She couldn't believe that love felt so good, so right -- and he was so fine. They went to church together. Where had he been all of her life? She wondered. She knew that it had to be a good thing; maybe the God that her mother talked about was coming through for her. They talked about God, family and how hard it was growing up when others thought they were different. She found out later that James joined the choir because she was there and it was a way to meet her. He could only sing a little but they didn't care because they were singing for the Lord, according to the choir director.

They were in LOVE and everything was perfect. One day they were walking home from choir rehearsal and on the way they stopped by the brook to rest, when he kissed her. Wow her first kiss; and one thing led to another. She didn't know what was going to happen next, only that it felt good. She was on cloud ten for months. After each rehearsal they repeated that wonderful intimate moment. This was the best kept secret she ever had. When they departed their secret place she slowly walked home savoring every moment of his kiss, his warm embrace, and his wonderful manly smell. She would have a hard time composing herself as she reached the long driveway. She kept repeating to herself, get yourself together, calm down, and fix your hair and clothes because Mother must never know!! One day she came home all happy and Nana asked her what had she been doing for the last few months after choir rehearsal with James? Of course she said nothing, but her wise mother said something that made her think she had eyes that followed her every move; "What you are doing will not end good, you are going to have a baby and he's going to leave you." She laughed and told her mother, "Impossible," but two weeks later she was late and pregnant, just as Mother said.

Looking back, she had lost her innocence, the most precious thing she had in life. She thought this would only happen on their wedding night, but it didn't. She also thought that it would have been his first time as well, but it wasn't. She thought it would be pleasurable but it wasn't, it hurt and she bled.

Now how was she going to explain this to her mother who never misses any details? How could something that feels so right end up so wrong and lead to such a mess? The secrets keep piling up.

He told her over and over he loved her. Two months afterwards he left and didn't stand by her. He joined the military and didn't come back for years. When Big Red found out that Alice was pregnant he told James, "No son of his was going to marry some no good, black as tar woman. You're too good to be married to the likes of her." And he forbid James to see her again. During those times you didn't disobey your parents. Big Red said he would get rid of her first before he allowed him to waste his life on a low life like her. James had no choice but to leave, so he told her that if he couldn't be with her he didn't want to be around. Alice questioned whether she mattered to him? Why didn't he stay and fight for her or take her away like they had planned?

James was completely different and not controlling like his father. He was a gentle, kind man and a good listener and lots of fun. Alice thought he cared but later questioned where she could have gone wrong. Was she that naive or just plain stupid? Everything she had learned in church, everything her Mom taught her, gone. After three months of dating she was pregnant.

Alice was left to bear the shame of being pregnant, unwed, and a Christian. She was wounded, empty, and her esteem was lower than ever. After being rejected and abandoned, she had a hard time accepting that her family loved her and wanted to keep her close, but that wasn't enough. All those suppressed feelings came flooding back. It's one thing to be rejected by people who don't have a vested interest in you, but when you are rejected and abandoned by the one who said and showed he loved you, it sent you to a deep dark place. Alice became angry at everyone; her mother for not telling her about men, sex and what to expect; her father for not making him marry her or at least stay and support her and the baby; instead he said, "You don't need anyone who don't want you, God loves you and will protect you." That may have been true but she didn't want God's love and protection. Alice wanted James, the love of her life. How was she to go on without him? She was ashamed, how could she hold her head up? How could she bring that shame upon her father, the Pastor? How could she stay and look her loving and kind mother in the eye and see the hurt in her heart. Her shame then turned to anger.

She was angry to the point she hated James. He promised he would be with her forever, instead he had left her pregnant with his baby to face everyone alone; all those who hated her and all those who had great expectations of her. Lastly, she was angry at God, the one her parents said to "have faith in, and he will protect you." Well, where was God and his protection for her from this? Alice felt she had faithfully gone to church every Sunday and all the other times. She had been a good girl all this time. Where was God when she needed him the most? She had so much anger, hurt, and was wounded inside; she left home.

Months after Sally was born, a lady who knew Pops was working in the shelter where Alice was living with Sally. Without Alice knowing it, she called Pops and Nana. With excitement they came to get Alice and Sally to take them home. Alice had hit a record low but not low enough to return home. She sent Sally back and gave her parents custody of her. Her parents kept Sally until she could get on her feet. She fell deeper and deeper into depression. Pops and Nana kept praying she would have a change of heart and come home. Soon afterwards Alice came to her senses and realized that she couldn't continue on that path. She had no money, no job, no hope, no choice, and the one person that kept her going was Sally. As long as she had Sally she had a little piece of James left to hold on to, so she returned home. Having the unconditional love from her parents allowed her to see that she was lovable regardless of her mistakes. She returned to God and back to church. She was still wounded and empty; however, a work in progress.

She was emotionally and spiritually open and an easy prey for the next smooth talker. Sure enough, three years down the bumpy road he came along and she fell into the next man's clutches and found herself pregnant again. Leroy left Alice high and dry; said that he didn't want to be tied down to a woman with one kid, another on the way and how could he be sure that this was his baby. Alice was strong enough to stay but too wounded to fight. She waited because waiting was all she could do. Leroy pretended that she didn't exist and he told everyone he had not been with her in that way.

Pops, Alice's father was a loving, responsible, kind and humble man. Pops hated that Alice was in this situation again. A part of him wanted to take matters into his own hands, but God would not be pleased. However, every Sunday he sat on the mourner's bench with thoughts of anger, rage, and murder. There was no amount of torture that he could inflict that would be equal to what Leroy, James and Big Red had done to his Baby girl. Nana overheard him say one day out of anger, "I should dump them in the river and kill um, just kill um." Once again there was nothing he could do; he questioned where he had gone wrong with raising his daughter and what he could have done differently. He blamed himself and became angry and withdrawn. Pops could only love Alice and that wasn't enough. This was his only daughter and he didn't know how to help her. Alice wondered why these two men had left her wounded and broken to defend herself. Watching Alice work through the pain of her wrong choices was difficult, but he knew that at the end of working through the struggles of life it always made you strong.

Leroy tried to keep it hush-hush but anyone who saw Sally knew she was James's. Leroy decided to stop running from the truth and accept responsibility for his child. Leroy married Alice and accepted both children as his. Alice mistakenly thought if he accepted her and Sally he must really love her. And maybe he did in his own selfish and controlling way. His jealousy and insecurity always caused fights after any of his male friends came by to visit. He covered up the insecurity by controlling everything Alice did. Having a father for her children cost Alice her peace of mind and the freedom to live. But she kept her struggles and fight to herself. Another secret she could not tell her father or her mother.

It was then that she began to understand what her mother was trying to teach her about the mercy and grace of God. The first thing Nana said to Alice was, "God loves us so much that he gave his only begotten Son to die a painful death that we might be saved. As hard as things may seem, God never turns his back on us, we turn away from him. But if we go to God and sincerely ask for forgiveness we will find that he is right there were we left him. God will pour that which we don't deserve, his grace and his mercy upon us. Alice went to the very spot where she lost her innocence and cried unto the Lord, and he forgave her. She developed a personal relationship with the Lord and he became her Lord and Savior. She learned that no matter how bad things were, if she stopped and put her trust in God he would direct her path.

She forgave all those that mistreated her and those she hurt because she was hurt. Interesting enough, when we are hurting we only want to make others hurt as bad as us. That kind of pain is so destructive. That kind of pain will also make you run to God and seek his help; but when we get free do we stay free or do we think we have arrived, let our guards down, and stop doing what we need to do to maintain? For every breakthrough there will come a day of testing, and if we have not maintained we will fall in the same ditch again. Alice did get free and was sincere, but longed for that warm embrace. The one and only thing she could never get from her father.

ANOTHER BIG SECRET

One day Alice, Sally and her sister came home and found Leroy in bed with the neighbor. Sally said to herself, "This lady was supposed to be Mom's friend. Her daughters, my sister and I played together. How could she do such a thing and call herself a friend? Now we know why she was always around, smiling in our face. How could he do such a thing?" Sally recalled the argument he and her Mom had before leaving. Mom wanted him to go with us and he refused, said he had stuff to do, "So go on about your business and do like you always do, stay all day." We thought he was just being mean, but he had other plans.

This is what happened, we decided we would be nice and return home early and surprise him. We should have surprised him and walked in but Mom didn't want my sister and me in the middle of their mess. Wow, she was never so wrong; we were right in the middle, top and bottom. The look on her face was devastating. It was one thing for him to slap a woman on her butt or place his hands elsewhere, but this had gone too far. They never discussed anything that their father did. It remained a secret, locked in the storage bins of their minds.

Sally wasn't sure if her mom told him what they had seen. They often had arguments that led to fights. Usually Alice was being accused of going behind his back with his male friends, doing what he was doing, but didn't know that we knew. Sally wanted to tell her father many times what they had seen but realized he would deny it. Nevertheless, it wouldn't have made a difference in his behavior. Alice said she never wanted to return to that dark empty place that almost took her life when James left her. However, what she had not realized was by being locked in an abusive marriage she was still in a deep dark place with nowhere or no one to go to or trust. She had stopped going to church because he would not let her go out, for fear that she would meet a man. The reality was he didn't want anyone to see the black eyes and bruises on her body. He was so insecure, which made him even more controlling. He controlled everything and everyone. That combination of insecurity, jealousy, and control will lead you down a very dangerous path.

Sally was not allowed to date because he didn't want her to turn out like her mom. He would tell her she was fast and high strung; whatever that meant. How would he know, if she wasn't allowed to have a boyfriend or date? It was just another way of controlling everyone.

Many years later after Alice had married Leroy, James returned home. Alice thought she had moved on but she still loved James. He never married and still loved her and had hoped that she had done the same. She asked herself, "Why didn't he write, call and tell her to wait for him until he came back?" Consequently, she realized that she had left those issues in her life unresolved and she never had forgiven him for leaving. She could not move on in life until she resolved all that pain that she had. All those unanswered questions were again questions that needed answers. But how could she get the answers knowing that if Leroy saw them together he would kill her. There was no way he would be able to face the reality of what he had always accused her of doing. She couldn't risk telling James that Leroy was physically abusive. She knew that Leroy would kill him. However, it would be more detrimental to her if she told Leroy and he didn't or wouldn't care. She didn't know what to do. She wanted to run into his arms but she dared not, this time the cost would be her life.

Sally didn't know that there was a secret buried so deep that involved her, and her past, present and future could change. Does she risk the exchange of confusion, disarray, and turmoil that she now lives, not knowing what she will come home to every day for the possibility of joy and happiness with her real father? They had never talked about the first three years of her life and who her father was, she just assumed it was Leroy. Would she, could she still love and respect her Mom for what was done? Would she hate that there has been a secret between them?

Sally was so young, how could I have explained it to her, Alice questioned? She wondered if she told James would he want to be a part of Sally's life or abandon her also? How would Leroy respond? There are some secrets maybe that are best left alone.

Oh, but the secret did get out. During Sally's high school years one of her so called friends told her who her real father was. Devastation wasn't the word for how she felt. How would she survive during the school day carrying this news, who was this man? All the things she thought would happen, short of her physically dying, happened and more. Sally asked her Mom if it was true, and how could she have withheld this information, where had this man been all her life, why wasn't he around and what had happened to keep him away from her?

Leroy was the only dad she knew, now what? Now she understood why he was so controlling over her. He knew this day may come and he would lose her, as he should, after all the hell they had gone through. For the first time Sally trusted God for herself, as she withheld this information from Leroy until she was sure as to what God wanted her to do. Months later, with God's strength, Sally talked to her Mom about how to tell Leroy she wanted an opportunity to meet her father. Controlling as expected, he told her she only has one father and was forbidden to see or speak of that no good man who left her and her mother. He went on to remind her of how good she had it and no father would have done what he had done for her.

At first that was okay because she really didn't want to have anything to do with him. He had hurt her Mom and there was enough hurt in their life. There is however, something that happens inside you when you are told what you can't have and eventually you look for it with all out determination.

Two years later, during her first year in college, she found out that James was keeping track of her. She had prayed about seeing him again and this time God said that it was time for her to forgive him and move on. Sally thought that would be the end of that, but you know God; after you start on the journey he will inform you that there is more required. She not only had to forgive James, but it was now time to develop a father-daughter relationship with him. Sally found out why Alice loved him, he was still that loving and caring man she met years ago. She forgave him also. Her Mom wasn't able to be a part of his life, but she was all her father had, so they kept their relationship to themselves. By them living in another state it was somewhat easy. They were so very close; he would sit and listen to all of her stories like he did with her Mom. He made her laugh; she finally had a father who really loved and cared about her, and made her feel like a little girl again. What she did not know was that he would die soon after they would become so close. After two years of healing, restoration and then enjoying her father's embrace, his zeal for life, he was everything to her; she had to now prepare for his death. He abruptly left her life as he did coming in her life.

"How could he just walk out of my life again?" Sally cried. No one knew he had become the real father she had longed for all her life. He was her joy, her inspiration, and now he was her best kept secret. How could she go on without him in her life, but she had promised James that she would not linger in unproductive grief, but finish her last semester of school and get her degree in honor of him. So she put the pain in a secret compartment and cried herself back to school. Sally graduated from college two months after James's death.

THE CIRCLE OF LIFE

She met a man at church who was nice and they had fun together. His name was TJ, and he introduced her to a different world. She still longed for her father. In the process he opened the door to her heart that had been shut since James's passing. And she didn't realize that she was looking for a father in TJ. She felt that she was in a worldwind trying to separate her feelings. She didn't want to hurt TJ knowing he cared for her, but she keep hearing her father say, "Think with your head not your heart or the burning desires of the flesh." There was also something inside of her that kept screaming, "Don't go down the same road like your Mom." She wanted to be needed and loved unconditionally. Was that possible or just wishful thinking and her bubble would soon be popped?

It was Thanksgiving night; Sally and TJ were returning to her home from his family's holiday dinner. The night was warm, the stars were out, so they stopped to take a walk around the lake. It was such a romantic night and for the first time she saw TJ for the wonderful man he was. He wasn't just the man who had helped her through the death of her father. But something had changed, she didn't know what or when, but she was happy. She, for the first time wanted to experience intimacy. In her head she started to plan her wedding and her wedding night. She could see it: the right place, the tender touch, and the warm embrace of her husband; how perfect it would be. TJ had other plans which included the right now. What happened? If I had only gotten out of dream land and back to reality, Sally thought. What was she thinking; what was TJ doing? But not now, not yet, she was speechless. Why here, why now, and why me? Was she doomed to follow in her mother's footsteps? One month later Sally found out that on Thanksgiving night she became pregnant. Sally longed for her father to talk to and help her make the right decision.

After 12 weeks Sally told TJ that she was pregnant. He was hurt and angry that she had held the information all this time without including him in the process. Equally, he was frightened all the same. He loved her but didn't want to be stuck in an obligated, committed relationship. TJ said he wasn't ready for marriage or to be a father, and he, too, walked out of my life. There she was living out her Mom's mistakes. She couldn't share the news with her parents because her stepfather, Leroy, would blame her Mom and he probably would beat Alice for her mistake. There was no way Sally would allow that to happen to her Mom. The decision was easy at that point. She had to have an abortion.

It was now the last day in the last week to legally perform an abortion. The suction procedure was the only one they could do during those days. Sally said they never prepared her for what she heard, felt and experienced. She could hear and feel the machine pulling, sucking, and ripping the baby apart limb by limb. One of them said softly, "It's a boy." The pain was overbearing. What happened next was even more devastating and demoralizing.

As they sat Sally up she was devastated by seeing all the blood. However, what was demoralizing was seeing the baby parts in the trash at the foot of the bed and knowing it was a boy child. It was as if they had identified the sex not because they knew, but to hurt her. They left the bloody parts there for her to see, she thought, so she would never come back again, and they were painfully right, she cried. The only reprieve was knowing she had to do this for her Mom. Once again she couldn't go to her Mom and cry on her shoulder. Another secret, when and where does it all end?

A year later TJ came back into Sally's life and convinced her that he needed her in his life, and six months later they were married.

At first she thought she had escaped the generational curse of men who were controlling, manipulating, having multiple affairs, and being physically abusive. TJ wasn't that type, but because of her insecurities, the hurts and pains that were connected to her past had jeopardized their marriage. She didn't see him, she saw her father cheating on her mother, and how he would beat her for speaking her mind. Her mother's pain became her pain. Her mother's rejection was now her rejection. Unlike Mom, she tried to leave him, but God wouldn't release her from the marriage because she had not done all that He had required of her. Sally had not done what she had told her parents they needed to do for God to repair their marriage. She was trapped between the mistakes of her parents' past and the emotional trap of her insecurities; lack of trust and faith.

The only thing that held her together was when they both went to church and rededicated their lives to the Lord. God taught her how to trust in the Lord and to forgive completely. She also realized that her marriage was under an attack. This attack is called "generational curse," and the enemy chooses families which he can tie one to the other with similar problems and destroy each one in the blood line. Satan, the enemy, hates forgiveness followed by salvation, followed by obedience; these are the only things that destroy the curse. As she grew in the Lord, she became more and more free of all the insecurities, lack of trust and faith in herself, her husband, her father and men in general.

Regardless of the situation, trust in the Lord and He would direct her path. Finally, learning that God had a plan for our lives, but we had to forgive in order to be forgiven and be restored to a right relationship with God. God's plan can and will then be revealed.

Looking back over our lives we see that what is done in secret always comes to the light. We all must come to the same realization that if we don't have a relationship with the Lord we can't find healing, restoration or restitution when dark hurtful secrets are uncovered.

Everything that happens to us is purposed for our lives. That was the purpose by which Christ died; if not we make His dying in vain. Being in alignment according to God's will for our lives allows us to count everything we go through as joy (James 1:1). We just need to follow God's road map and not detour. Detours are Satan traps, but when Christ has set us free, stand firm and do not get entangle again (Gal 5:1).

CHAPTER 4

FLIP THE SCRIPT

Women, we like to think that all of our problems are male related. However, in my years of experience five angry men put together is no match for one scornful woman. Yes, men are strong and can be self-centered, however, study shows that men view life from a very tunnel vision view point, where women view from an open view point. Men focus on what is ahead, straight to the point, bottom line and women focus on relationships, what and who are around her and how she can bring them into her world. In many marriages and relationships today women are not treated as equal partners. However, a woman can make or break a man and make or break a marriage. She has an innate ability to persuade, which is very powerful.

Most men never plan on having an affair, they plan to have good sex. Women have affairs first and the good sex is an added bonus. If she is planning to step out on her husband she would choose carefully who she plans to allow to come into her world. Her reasoning for exploring outside of her safety zone falls under these three categories. The first, she has been hurt, unappreciatcd, and lonely. This woman has made a conscious decision, if he can... She's not going to sit at home and wait for a change, she's going to have to find someone who will appreciate her for her. This way of thinking will change her entire life and her perspective. This woman is looking for a relationship, and if her significant other doesn't recognize the sign she closes the door of her heart; he will lose her forever.

The second type of woman has been hurt by many men and is tired of the game, so she begins to play the game too. She could care less about a relationship, she learned how to play the game from the game master, except she has now flipped the script. Because she was created with emotions she has more charm, more appeal and knows how to work her stuff. She will get in and out before he knows what hit him. She is devious and cunning with a kiss. The kiss of death! Her motives are only to destroy and take down every man that comes in contact with her.

The third is the one who, too, doesn't want a relationship. She doesn't have the time or the energy required for a committed relationship. For her it doesn't matter if he is single, married or in a relationship, she only wants a good time, and if you last a week or a month count yourself lucky.

These women are found in every walk of life, however, the more money and power she has the more devious and dangerous she can become. Throughout history this woman has been called Jezebel. Jezebel had money, power and control. What Jezebel wanted she got, and to get it she didn't care who she walked on or over. Control is her game, not because of insecurity but for the need for power. Let me share the stories of some of these women: the first is Bertha – Controller, then there's Dee – High Maintenance, followed by Tina – Who's Needy, Victoria – The Gold Digger, and finally, Darlene – Have It All and Don't Want It.

Bertha the Controller

Bertha said she had no idea she was controlling. From a child up her friends told her, "Don't be so controlling," and she would respond, "I'm not controlling, I'm a leader and a leader must lead. My Momma was a leader and I learned to be a leader like her."

Let me tell you about me. I was a criminal attorney and a partner in my Mom's firm. My father was a heart surgeon. As I became older my leadership skills were always needed. I couldn't believe there were so many people who couldn't do simple things and needed my expertise. As an attorney I helped everyone out of their dilemma, but they paid dearly for my expertise. And of course when I found my husband, he was someone who I could mold and shape the way I wanted him to be. I could create the man of my dreams and then pull his strings whenever I needed him to perform for me. He was so young and naive. I was his first; can you believe that, a 28 year old virgin just right for the picking. I had molded, created, and shaped him into a fine respectable businessman. I gave him all the things he dreamed of having. Two years later, when I was sure he was in a position where he needed me and what I could offer him, I gave him an ultimatum; either marry me or pay half of everything that I had purchased for him. During the start up of his business I had him sign a prenuptial agreement for the car, house, boat, jewelry and the vacation property that I had purchased and allowed him to enjoy. It stated that if after two years we didn't get married he would have to pay fifty percent of those things that he enjoyed, and sixty to seventy percent of anything he claimed ownership. As a lawyer I knew how to write a contract, and hid what I wanted to in the fine print. I didn't hand-pick, dress, teach him to be respectable, get him a better job so he wouldn't embarrass me for nothing. I had too much invested in him for him to walk out the door.

What was he going to go back to, being just a construction worker? Because the company he owned was also mine. So he did the right thing, married me. All he had to do was to look good, sound intelligent when we went out and perform on demand, otherwise, he could do whatever he wanted. He had the best of both worlds.

Somehow he did something and I became pregnant. I hated him for fifteen months and during that time he stayed far away from me. The day my son took his first step into his Daddy's arms and not mine, I realized I had better change my method because they were about to flip the script on me. So I pretended to love him, and he loved me back unconditionally. Why, I don't know, because I treated him like he was my pathetic slave and I dangle him like a puppet. However, I was the one who got "got".

During an argument one day, as usual I threaten to discard him like trash and he flipped the script. He told me that he didn't need me to survive and that he had his name taken off all the things that I had used for leverage to control him. He went on to say that he would be better off without me, that he only stayed because he loved me and knew that I didn't know how to love a real man, but was beginning to change. He then gave me an ultimatum, change or be left by myself, and their son would be with him. He gave me a look that I've never seen before and then said, "Baby you'll look for us and we will be gone. We will hit the road jack and won't come back no more, no more." How could he just flip the script on me, how and when did I lose control? I stayed and began to work on changing me. His love was so pure and genuine that once I got over being angry I could appreciate the real man that I had in him. Yes, I thought I was molding him into a man, however, quite the opposite happened, I learned that he was helping me find the real woman he saw in me under all the mess.

Once again I was pregnant. This time we had a daughter and she was even more lovable. I began to notice I had become nicer to my husband and we were enjoying each other. I was losing control, but enjoying life. To this day I haven't figured out how he did it or what he did. He said he put me in God's hands, and the rest is history.

One day he asked me to go to church, but of course I wasn't going to have some man and his church control me, my money, or my emotions. Besides, it doesn't take two and an half hours and all that jumping up and falling out, messing up a $100 hairdo to show off for man. I turned around with my hands on my hips and told him, "I wasn't about to replace my god with his God whom I didn't know or see. I had plenty of love and money, so why did I need his God?"

He didn't say anything for the rest of the week and again something happened beyond my control. I awakened, dressed and went to church with my family. Every Sunday for a month I went, and he never asked me except for that one time. If he would just argue with me, but he didn't, he never did. I use to think he was a wimp, but the bottom line was he had more control than I ever did, his power rested in the God he served.

The lawyer in me had to put God to the test, but he taught me through his Word how to love and forgive, have compassion, mercy and grace. I surrendered my life to the Lord, and in exchange I relinquished the control in every area of my life, and I am now an advocate for husbands and wives working as a team. I also destroyed the prenuptial agreement file and reinforced a covenant relationship as equal joint owners. I am so thankful for the loving husband that the Lord put in my life, for me to know that without God I was nothing, but with God I have life abundantly. Today I am a glorious woman of God. It was not our doing, it was God's.

Dee The High Maintenance Woman

Dee is my name, you taking care of me is my game. You see it was like this growing up, we were poor. My grandma struggled, my momma struggled, my auntie struggled, my sister struggled; I came from a long list of women who struggled alone. I was determined I wasn't going to follow in their footsteps. I watched how the other girls carried themselves, how they walked, talked, ate; what activities got them ahead, and I was smart. I stayed to myself so no one would suspect what I was doing, not even my family. They thought I was a bookworm.

The first year in high school was my coming out year. I made sure that I hung with the right kind of girls. I looked the part and talked their talk. I moved from just being a cheerleader to being the captain of the squad. I dated the captain of the football team, not because he was the captain but because he could afford my wants.

My parents' financial status and my 4.0 GPA got me in the best college on an all-expenses paid scholarship. I went to school for Business Management and later became a legal secretary. I was too busy learning how not to be a house maid and Mom was happy one of us was going to make it out of the projects, so I never learned how to do the basic things like cook, clean or wash clothes.

I only dated men who could afford my tastes. I enjoyed eating out because I couldn't cook. I allowed you to spend the week with me if you were going to clean my apartment and wash my clothes. David and I had such a great understanding; I married him. The agreement was he would work the night shift at the hospital, that way he was home in the day to clean, wash and have dinner on the stove. When I needed something extra like a new car, vacation, or a fur, he would work overtime and I would take him out for dinner. My job was to look good for him; my hair, nails, and my shape. I wore only designer clothes and shoes and purchased the same for him. He drove an SUV and I drove a BMW 800 series.

Life was great until the hospital downsized and laid off half of the lab technicians. After six months of David sitting around doing nothing except handing out excuses, I became angry. I needed a vacation and a new car and he couldn't deliver. He started drinking because he couldn't stand my bickering. He called me selfish, self-centered and an egotistical spoiled brat. However, he forgot I wasn't the one who changed, I was that way when he married me, so why change now just because he was too lazy to get a job. David told me to shape up or ship out. Boy, those were the wrong words and for the first time in my life I cleaned house. I packed him up and threw him out so fast he needed a drink.

I thought I would be happy his sorry behind was gone, but as it turned out the sorry one was me, and I needed him more than he needed me. I didn't know how to do anything. I was eating out two or three times a day, taking all my clothes to the laundry, spending money on hair, nails, clothes, and the gym, but couldn't balance a checkbook. I was a mess, my life was a mess. I was evicted and my car was repossessed before I saw what I had become. I couldn't blame anyone but me. I had become my own worst enemy.

David told me some years later it hurt him to have to watched me hit bottom, but that was the only way I would see who and what I had become. I wish I didn't have to lose everything, including my marriage in order to see. He said that behind that wall was a loving person, he just couldn't reach her. He had to leave me to find my way on my own. David and I remained friends, he loved me too much to go back to a codependent relationship, he said. I am still working on me and hoping maybe one day it will be safe for him to be my husband again.

Needy Tina

I'm Tina and I too have struggled all my life with being accepted by others. I came from a good Christian home, both parents and one older brother and a younger sister. I always felt that I could never do anything as well as my brother and sister. They made straight A's and I made C's. They played an instrument, they had great voices and were liked by all, but not me. They married and are happy, and I am single and alone and lonely.

I tried to figure out why I always get walked on and taken advantage of. I help any and everyone that I feel needs my assistance. I have given food and money even when it meant that I had to do without, or had my utilities turned off. However, when I need help there's no one for me.

Men use me and leave me. They say they love me but there's always something that hinders them from committing. After I help them get on their feet they keep walking.

One day after fasting and praying for thirty days, the Lord showed me that I was too needy, and my neediness was pushing people away. The spirit of need has some attachments; they are the spirit of self-centeredness, loneliness, low self-esteem, and complaining. The reason I will give my last and beyond is due to a co-dependent relationship that has developed out of need. What I really want to do is say, "No, go get your own, go home, do for yourself, and it's not okay that I give my last and be without."

God asked me what would happen if I stopped helping everyone so I could help myself. I told him they would be angry, find another way and not be my friend until there was another crisis in their life. If I continued to bail them out of crisis after crisis but not take the advice to not repeat the crisis, what have they learned?

Tina had to learn that family and those who are the closest to her are the ones who will use you until they ring you dry and still come back for more and more. They don't understand "no," because I don't know how to say it, and say it consistently in love. It wasn't until I got sick and was hospitalized for a month; no one could get anything from me but survived without my help, that I saw I wasn't as needed.

Victoria the Gold Digger

Well hello Darling, my name is Victoria. I'm what they call a gold digger and I am proud to be one. I have been in four relationships and they all were steps to get me where I am today. I am very tall with long thin legs, blossoming breasts, just right curved hips and long black hair. I knew how to sit, walk, look and bend that would have men drooling. I knew what worked and I worked what I knew. I wasn't in the relationship for a relationship or love, but to get me where I needed to be on the social ticket. I wanted the fame, the name, the money and all the bells and whistles that came along with it. There's no time in my plan to get tied down with family gatherings and children. I get in and get out. I would find the older lonely man about to kick the bucket, or the young one who just wants someone who makes him look good. I go in with an agenda to marry, gain as much assets and money as I can, and roll out. If I stay too long and get involved in family drama, meet parents who just might like me and I like them back, building a relationship, someone may get hurt, resulting in long divorce ligations. I planned to always keep the relationship cordial, public, and non engaging. We would have sex, not love making; lust not passion; and we would have an understanding, not intimacy.

The first relationship lasted one year. He was a wealthy man in his seventies and I was his 23 year old receptionist. Within the first month I knew what he was worth and what he wanted. I gave him all of that and more. I moved from being his receptionist to his assistant. Four months later I had persuaded him to turn the business over to his partner, and we could travel while he took some much needed time to strengthen his heart. He did, and we were engaged and married by the sixth month, and honeymooning in Europe for a month. I knew that he had heart problems from working as a temp for his heart doctor. Too much stress on the heart would be fatal and I knew just how to love him to death.

He had never been married because he was all about building his dental business. He had twelve offices and they all were thriving. He didn't need to work but he enjoyed what he did, he only took time off to play golf. I made sure he had a smile on his face twenty four seven. His older friends wanted to know how they could find a woman like me. Every now and then he allowed me to play with them.

As he was on his way to the other side of life, I was lining up the next prey. One year later on our anniversary, I took him sky diving. After a plane ride filled with hot and heavy romance, we put on the parachutes and dove into the sunset. That was the last item on his wish list and that one took him out. I cried all the way to the bank and into his best man's arms.

His best friend was a tall, good looking defense attorney at his firm, and like his friend had heart problems, which was repaired by implanting a pace maker. The only difference was he was in good shape and he worked out daily. I knew I would have my work cut out for me, but I was up to the challenge.

We were married soon after the reading of the will. I enjoyed the lime life, dinners, conferences and social networking. This marriage put me in the social status where I wanted to be, therefore, I didn't mind taking a little more time in this marriage.

He was working on a high profile case, and one day on the way from court he was shot. I remember thinking how wonderful these two years were and how nicely I was rewarded for good behavior. He left me everything he had and I was well compensated. By now I had accrued two houses in the States and one in Europe; investments, stocks, bonds and the shareholder of two businesses and more.

You would think I had enough to quit and settle down. But it had become a way of life for me. I married again to a younger man who demanded more of me. We were divorced a year later.

Husband four was Brock. He was different from all the other men I had married. He pressured me, he kindled the relationship, he loved me and for the first time I returned the love. He wasn't a wealthy man, didn't own a business nor wanted to. He was a professor at the university. We would get together and talk. I never talked with the others, but he had a way of touching my heart and taking an interest in who I was and what I needed and wanted in life. No one had ever taken the time to know me, but he did. He didn't care about my money or wealth, he cared about me. For the first time I loved someone other than me. He taught me how to love unconditionally and I was happy and content.

We did everything together, including having a family. I realized I had missed out on the best part of a relationship. God never intended marriages to be a business contract but a covenant relationship. Husbands must love their wives as Christ loves the church and wives be submissive to their husband. Submission simply means to come in agreement with him and walk as one, not two separate entities. I learned so much by being with Brock. He showed me that without Jesus as the center of your life it is impossible to love anyone, including ourselves. I couldn't love because I was incapable of love. But when Brock introduced Jesus to me, it was the best thing that ever happened in my life. I opened my heart and allowed Christ to help me make lasting changes in my life. We have been married for twenty years and each year gets better and better.

Darlene – I Had It All and Didn't Want It

Let me introduce myself to you. I'm 40, married with two children, both in middle school and have been honor roll students since first grade. My kids are very active in school, community activities and church. My husband, Scott, is a hard-working man who would and has done anything for our family and me. There was a time when I was sick for a long time and the doctors didn't know what was wrong. My husband worked, cared for the children and the high demand of their schedules, maintained the house and loved me even more. The more demanding the load became, the more joy he seemed to have doing what was required. I wanted to get my Mom or someone to come and help but he continuously said, "I got it," and he did.

My Mom did come, but that wasn't until I had to have surgery and she was there with me. Scott's an X-ray technician at the hospital and the hospital was up for their yearly certification. The surgery came during this time, which is a critical time and no one could take leave. We were happy that Mom was there to give him a break and he was grateful for her help.

It took me a year to improve physically. However, something happened to my spirit. You would think

I would be ever grateful, but I wasn't. The longer I stayed in the bed the more bitter I became. The kinder my husband was to me the colder I became. I had become so cold and bitter that my Mom had become so tired of talking to me about my attitude until she couldn't take it any longer and went home. I didn't want the marriage, family, church or anything. How could my life be so turned upside down, so messed up, and where do I go from here?

Somehow I was able to get a job with the company I had worked for. Six months after returning I ran into an old friend and we began to take our lunch together. I found myself dressing up and looking forward to our time together. He had put the spark back in my life. I loved my husband but I was drawn to my old friend. My husband asked why I seemed different. I couldn't tell him I wanted out of the marriage.

Shortly after, the day came when I moved out and left everything I value behind. It didn't take long before I found out the same man who had enticed me and fed me hope was beating me and stealing from me. He never told me that he was married. He never told me that he was dealing drugs and needed my place to run his drug business. What had I done? How did I manage to give up everything and end up with nothing? Could I go home? Would they take me back? How do I put aside my hurt and pride to crawl back? How do I face my church? How do I face God?

One night I awakened and the apartment was full of smoke, drugs and men. I was afraid for my life. I made three calls; I called God first and asked for protection and a way out of this mess that I was in. Second, the police, who came and locked all of them up and took me to a shelter. My apartment had become a crime scene. The third call was to my husband. He came to the shelter the next day and took me to my Mother's. After a year of counseling and working hard to rebuild the trust, we got back together.

For some of us God has to allow us to lose everything for us to realize the wonderful gift he had given us in the beginning. I am so thankful for a second chance. Our marriage and family is stronger. I now teach women about the downfall of being depressed and how to find themselves in the midst of the rubble.

Understanding and embracing your role as a man and a woman individually, and as one, will allow you to begin to focus on the big picture that God has created for marriage, and to bear all, not just the fruit and blessings. Then the relationship can be based on mutual love, trust and respect resulting in genuine consideration for one another.

CHAPTER 5

COUNT THE COST

The attitude and conditions of women have changed a great deal since the earlier seventies. Many of us started out in loving obligated marriages, not knowing what marriage required except being faithful and submissive wives. After many years we now have the opportunity and the freedom to express ourselves vocally, emotionally and sexually. As a result, marriage is no longer the pivotal part of relationships and family. Sex outside of marriage has become more popular regardless of its biblical incorrectness or morally improper. We have moved from believing in the institution of marriage to "I can do bad all by myself," and "I do whatever feels good." As couples and individuals we have ventured out socially and found that we were kept in darkness too long. What forces you in the dark? When and where did we lay down or trade the compass that was given us from the foundation of the world, for an imitation GPS. Many of us today would say the compass was too hard to read, it required too much time, knowledge and dedication. In looking for a quick and easy way to journey through life, we sell out to the enemy by purchasing the latest navigation system with all the bells and whistles. What we didn't know or even ask was that it was without the chip, and the power source was missing. It's amazing how many times we look at the outside of a person and think they are an intelligent, kind, caring individual but never once stop to examine the content. We mistakenly think we have obtained something or someone good until trouble slaps us in the face, and right in the midst of the mess we find out it was all a lie. After we have been hurt, abandoned, rejected, raped, we realize that the content was hard, cold and hollow, or filled with garbage and residue of what others have dumped into them.

Man and woman in the 3rd chapter of Genesis disobeyed God in the Garden of Eden by eating the forbidden fruit. God gave Adam a command in the garden, this was prior to the creation of Eve; "do not eat from the tree of knowledge and of good and evil" (2:7-18). Yes, Eve was lied to and tricked by the serpent to first test the validity of God's word. When nothing happened she took the fruit to Adam and said, "Look, nothing happened to me, the serpent must be right." Adam was right there beside her, not in the next garden. He could have prevented her from being enticed by the serpent, but he wanted to see, just like Eve, if what God had said was true or not. Satan planted the first seed of deception and Adam and Eve indulged. Because of their disobedience that seed remains planted, and we continue to indulge in the deceitful pleasures that slowly kill us. God had provided more than enough in just that one garden for them. Gen 2:9, states that God put in the garden all types of trees that were pleasurable to the eye and good for food. There was nothing lacking from their daily menu. Eve went against the nature of God by providing food for man. And we have been providing for men ever since. The Serpent told them that if they ate from the tree their eyes would be opened and they would be as knowledgeable as God, knowing good and evil. God never intended for us to ever experience evil. God instructed Adam as he walked in the cool of the garden of every living thing that was there, so he knew that the snake was a snake; crafty. Each living creature had a purpose so he had to have told Adam that the snake was crafty, because that is what God called him. Adam and Eve's disobedience led them to a place of nakedness, blame shifting, denial, shame, and sin. Their lives were transformed from blissfully bliss to generationally cursed. Immediately afterward their eyes were opened and they saw that they were naked. They covered up with fig leaves then hid from God. God asked, "Where are you and who told you that you were naked? What have you done?"

Let's get real and honest. We have been in darkness too long. There are eight signs that indicate we are in darkness. The following questions must be asked of ourselves and of our partners before we take the leap into a relationship, shack and shout, and most of all before marriage.

Do I or my mate:

1. stand by and watch hurtful things happen, knowing that it is harmful and do nothing to prevent it, and are not concerned about the consequences of wrong doing,

2. when you are physically, sexually or emotionally abused, excuses are made over and over but you continue to stay, out of fear,

3. you are the only one working hard to provide while your partner's laying around doing absolutely nothing,

4. you have lost your identity, values, self worth, self respect and are forced to function as told,

5. when your partner brings the other woman/man in your house, in your bed; or your child becomes the pawn to pay your rent, and you allow it because you've lost your fight and your control,

6. allow your partner to talk and treat your child like trash,

7. the need for control and being the center of attention demands that all relationships with family, friends and others must be severed,

8. instead of being full of life, you now feel like a sponge that has been squeezed dry.

If we answer "yes" to any of these, we need to evaluate if this is the person for us, before we commit. Too often we get involved and are bound for life. Death may be the only way out, whether, emotionally, spiritually or physically, so put your Reeboks on, run for your life and never look back.

It was intended that man and woman be one, that they walk together in agreement (Amos 3:3), there God is in the midst (Matt. 18:19). Since the garden, men and women have been in a rebellious state. We are constantly eating or touching the forbidden fruit only to find that our eyes aren't just open to what we do see, but to the things that we don't need to know, resulting in rebellion, rejection, disobedience, anger and bitterness. As a result, the 80's brought about the lowering of standards and moral fortitude being reduced to the bare minimum. An increase in the abuse of drugs, alcohol, sex, rape, incest, abortions, and divorce are a consequence of disobedience. God tells us in Isaiah 55:8 that His ways are not our ways and warns us not to be conformed to this world but be ye transformed by the renewing of your minds, Roman 12:2.

God had to do a complete makeover in the lives of his children. He first has to redeem us then teach us how to be in right relationship with him again. Whether we have veered off the path a little or a lot, the makeover was and is necessary. This makeover is even more extreme because we don't have the right concept of who we are outside of our made up, dramatized, fantasies that we have given birth to and allowed to mature. In the end we find the cruel reality that we have fallen far from the mark. From the start we were broken emotionally, socially, and spiritually. We, as a class of people, don't know who we are, where we've been or where we are going. Therefore, we lose our identity and we begin to take the identity of the person to whom we are enslaved. Consequently, we can't identify the brake or the origin. The outcome of two broken people who don't know themselves and come together, is the creation of a dysfunctional family. Will we allow the broken pieces of not knowing where we have come from to be repaired? Will we ever allow ourselves to be put on the potters wheel to be reshaped into something new and worthy of giving or receiving love? Are the walls that we put up to protect us so high and thick that no one can get in and we can't get out to receive healing, deliverance, and able to reach our destiny? Yes, we can. However, this extreme makeover again is unavoidable and painful because you have to look inside of self and not stop searching until you find the answer to the who, why, when, where and what happened questions.

Looking back over the years when asked again and again, what happened, it always stems back to the environment and background. Somewhere in their past the individual has been enslaved to something or someone. We may not be enslaved in chains and shackles as our forefathers were, but we continue to wear or do the things that are evidence of being enslaved; our large earrings, ankle chains, pants worn below our butts, the hard street attitude, provocative dress, drugs, alcohol and sex. So I ask you, can you identify your master? The stronger and healthier the men and women appeared, the more money was made in the slave trade. The price of our freedom is higher than ever, however we pay whatever is asked even if it means selling our children and their inheritance.

How far have we come? Parents and kids today are out of control, which makes it hard for those who want to make something of them. Today we have some of the best educational systems and opportunities to receive a higher education anywhere in America we choose. All the same, our youth either refuse to go to school, or don't care whether they, or anyone else, get an education. A few of the youth today find that school is only a social club where they can hang out, do drugs, get involved in gang activity, fight and cause trouble, and do everything except learn. To them, education is not wanted or needed, and they hinder and disrupt the process of those who do want to learn.

This behavior is the result of our young children looking for a sense of belonging, love and acceptance at home. Needless to say, they can't receive from their parents or guardians something that they themselves don't have. This is one of the reasons our children today have turned to the streets and/or are involved in gangs. Once they get involved in a gang they are in for life or death. The other deficiency in our families is attention, and both parent and children fight for it among each other. As a result, the cruel cycle of abuse, incest, rape and prostitution are on the rise.

Is being bound to a lifestyle more important than family values? Our ancestors taught us to protect the family and respect the family. We have changed our masters; still, we have not taken the chains off. We were identified as poor or low class people, never owning anything, no self worth, no values and no goals. Our fore parents did bring us up and out of the state that we were in at that time. They boycotted buses, marched in the street, fought for education and became important inventors, medical doctors, lawyers, and even teachers. They took pride in their families and fought hard to get free, and 130 years later we are bound again[2]. They taught their children the bible and passed down the legacy and history of where and how far they had come. Each generation thereafter have said they want to, or attempt to, fix or simplify "the hard lives" of our parents, and with each generation we have gone backwards to slavery. We are also slaves to the almighty dollar, the more we make the more we want. We want what we see and will get it without counting the cost. We become angry with others, not ourselves, if what we want is unattainable or our attempt fails. We teach our children we can never have enough, and we get upset when they ask repeatedly for things they can't have; but we taught them to never be satisfied. When bill collectors call we have taught them to lie. A driver cuts you off and you chase after them calling them every negative and degrading name possible. We jump in the face of anyone who looks at us wrong, even persons of authority, so we taught them not to respect others and those in authority. The law is broken in front of them; stealing, fighting, stabbing, killing, destroying others property, and to say the least, going to jail is a joke.

---

[2]   How does slavery affect black people today? African-American Forum, Larry 7D, Jacksonville, FL, March 9, 2007

We are now brainwashed into believing the opposite of our forefathers. We were either told we will never have anything, we can have it all, we have to have the best, the biggest or the most expensive; but again at what cost? We fall for every get rich quick scheme. The check is always in the mail but the mailman must have lost your address. Because we have never had anything of value, if and when we get it, we don't appreciate it or know how to take care of it. So, the more we reach to obtain, the more we lose what little we have. Only a fraction of the people who play and win the lottery millions have anything one year later, consequently, they are worse off than they were before they won. No one prospers from get rich drop from heaven, believe it receive it tricks. As a result, the person who falls victim of that additive behavior suffers more after losing the riches with withdrawals, guilt and depression.

Prosperity comes from God, yes, but through living an obedient, faithful and disciplined life. There is a world concept that states the more money one has the more power they acquire. We have to work two and three jobs to keep up with what society says we have to have. We have to have the biggest houses, best cars, designer clothes, and a lot of bling-bling; but pay a higher interest rate. The more we demand it the more it is supplied at a rate that we can't continue to pay. Yes, it's great that we have arrived but again, at what cost? We don't spend time with our spouses, family and children. Our children are raising themselves. Marriage and family requires consistent time and attention from someone not something. Relationships are maintained by what feels good; sex, money and control. Both individuals and couples must begin to take a stand, educate and discipline themselves, and take the time to make right and hard decisions. Take back the control from others, society and the enemy within ourselves.

The foreclosure rate has increased 45 percent[3] since August 2006, because we have become a slave to the bigger and better, but our bank account says no, not yet. Who cares for your children when you work all the time; the school system, the streets, the drug dealer, that nasty man whose been waiting for your daughters and sons to have his way. There are an estimated 20 percent of all black men born from 1965 through 1969 which have served time in prison by the time they reached their early 30's. Equally startling, 30.2 percent of those who didn't attend college had gone to prison by 1999,

---

[3] Relty Trac News and Events, Sept 2006

and 58.9 percent of blacks became high school dropouts. By the end of 1999, 1.3 million men were in federal or state prisons.[4] The National figure as of January 1, 2008, 1,596,127 people are in state and federal prison and 723,131 are in local jails. of that number 230 million are American adults. For men between the ages of 20 and 34, there is a 9 to 1 ratio of black men to white men in jail. The racial disparity for women also is stacked. One of every 355 white women age 35-39, compared to one of every 100 black woman of the same age are in prisons today.[5] Those arrested for drug offenses nearly tripled from 580,900 in 1980 to 1,579,566 by the year 2000. Four of every five drug prisoners are African-American (56%), and while drug use and abuse cuts across racial and ethnic categories; it has fallen disproportionately on low-income black communities with stiffer and longer sentencing than the white drug prisoner. So I continue to say we are still in bondage.

Anger, rejection, abandonment and abuse that has not been dealt with, the emotional effects are turned inward where we appear calm but are exploding on the inside, or expressed in an aggressive behavior

---

[4] Univ. of Washington Office of News and Information May 20, 2004, Social Science, Law and Policy

[5] 2008 The Associated Press

called acting out. This cycle of anger, bitterness and abusive behavior is because we get ourselves in a mess; we either go into denial, blame shifting, withdrawal, or do nothing, allowing a bad situation to become worst. Being asked to produce on every side for job, home, family, church and social life until there's nothing left, with no positive influences eventually will cause you to feel hopeless and desireless. This also leads to increased anger and bitterness because they feel they have no way of getting off the roller coaster. No one cares and all the doors shut much quicker than they open. Without making the necessary changes in your lifestyle will cause you to spiral out of control. The place called home, which should be a place of calm and resolve, has become the haunted house that has you locked down in bondage.

Many spouses are angry with their partners for abandoning them. They often wish they had run first and not be left with the responsibility and the guilt. This behavior is then covered up by denial, blame shifting, repression or suppression. Being asked to continue to be productive at work, home, church and in our social life with no positive influences eventually will cause a break down mentally, physically and psychologically.

The only way out is to fight; but we never fight the real enemy. The real enemy, "inner me," is in me. Somewhere in the midst of wanting to arrive where we had never been, we lost what had been accomplished; our self worth, dignity, self respect and a sense of purpose. Our wanting to be and do better has put us into spiritual and economical bondage because we don't live what we preach. This makeover must begin with us identifying that we are right where we are, at our lowest point and needing to be made over. Next, we have to realize we have tried everything and everything has failed, it is now time to do it God's way. We have to get rid of the old way of doing and living and put on a new way of living. (Who Am I - Worksheet – Appendix - 1)

In order to have that which we've never had, we have to be bold enough to do that which we have never done before. This also requires that we sit down with the address book, cell phone, or blackberry and start getting rid of baggage. Baggage can be recognized four ways: (1) they take and take and never give; (2) they are never around when you need them; (3) they are a liability and not an asset in your life; (4) they pull you down rather than build you up.

At some point in our lives God calls us into repentance, "Jesus answered and said unto him, Verily, verily, I say unto thee, Except a man be born again he cannot see the kingdom of God', Except a man be born of water and of the Spirit, he cannot enter into the kingdom of God. ⁶That which is born of the flesh is flesh; and that which is born of the Spirit is spirit. ⁷Marvel not that I said unto thee, you must be born again (John 3:3, 5-7). Jesus goes on to say *"That if thou shall confess with thy mouth the Lord Jesus, and shall believe in your heart that God hath raised him from the dead, thou shall be saved. For with the heart man believeth unto righteousness; and with the mouth confession is made unto salvation. For the scripture said, whosoever believeth on him shall not be ashamed. For there is no difference between the Jew and the Greek: for the same Lord over all is rich unto all that call upon him. For whosoever shall call upon the name of the Lord shall be saved. How then shall they call on him in whom they have not believed, and how shall they believe in him of whom they have not heard, and how shall they hear without a preacher? (Rm. 10:9-14)*

As Christians we have to stop toting and quoting the bible; seeking first the Kingdom of God and all these things will be added unto us, and become saints of God because he, Jesus, makes intercession for the saints according to the will of God. Therefore we have *"to study to show thyself approved unto God, a workman that needeth not to be ashamed, rightly dividing the word of truth" (2 Tim. 2:15), "living and applying his word line upon line and precept upon precept."* Every saint God will reckon with us, it may not be easy and it may not be quick. Just as it was a process by which we got into the mess, it is a process by which we come out, however, rest assure God's desire is for us to be reconnected, restored and every broken area of our messed up lives be repaired. Spending time in God's Word avails God to teach and equip us with the only authority that we have to live by, where by the standard doesn't change, (Matt. 28: 18-19). People, laws, policies and lifestyles change, but God and His Word never change, (Mal. 3:6, Heb. 7:21). *He is a God that he should not lie, (Numbers 23:19).* It is also the only authority we need to: *"be strong in the Lord, and in the power of his might. Put on the whole armour of God, that ye may be able to stand against the wiles of the devil. For we wrestle not against flesh and blood, but against principalities, against powers, against the rulers of the darkness of this world, against spiritual wickedness in high places. Wherefore take unto you the whole armour of God, that ye may be able to withstand in the evil day, and having done all, to stand. Stand therefore, having your loins girt about with truth, and having on the breastplate of righteousness; And your feet shod with the preparation of the gospel of peace; Above all, taking the shield of faith, wherewith ye shall be able to quench all the fiery darts of the wicked. And take the helmet of salvation, and the sword of the Spirit, which is the Word of God: Praying always with all prayer and supplication in the Spirit, and watching thereunto with all perseverance and supplication for all saints; And for me, that utterance may be given unto me, that I may open my mouth boldly, to make known the mystery of the gospel, For which I am an ambassador in bonds: that therein I may speak boldly, as I ought to speak" (Eph. 6:10-20).*

Men and women must become bold, holy and effective ambassadors for Christ, then we will be able to make a real difference in the Kingdom.

CHAPTER 6

TAKING BACK THE CONTROL

God please opens our eyes that we may see. So often I hear women say, "We are tired of going through, getting walked on, walked over, put down, used or misused." They blame God for not responding, not caring, not taking time to meet their needs, and that's why they are the way they are. God's reply is He is willing, able and available to help us. He's been knocking on our door with a way of escape but we aren't listening. We are so burdened down, stressed out, burned out, afraid and depressed that we couldn't hear Him if He was standing in front of us yelling for us to take His hand so he can lead us to a better place. This wall that we put up makes it impossible for Him to help. We want to make time for God, everyone and everything, but we, accomplish nothing. We sit down and fall asleep because our bodies are overwhelmingly tired. Upon waking up, everything is left undone; our family then looks us in the face like we have committed a crime or lost our mind. But everyone else is permitted to take a nap, a break, hang out and relax, except you. In order to continue to pour out you must stop and take care of you. All of us have had moments when we feel unappreciated, not loved or wanted, but do we care enough about ourselves to allow self love. We have to tell ourselves first, "I appreciate me, I love me and I want me for me, and if you don't like it that's your loss not mine."

I remember when I was the Director of my own counseling center, making almost equal my first husband's salary, but that wasn't good enough for him. He didn't value what I did, he felt counseling people who were hurting and helping individuals with problems was a waste of time. There were times I felt that I was living my childhood all over again by saying what my father would say to my mom and I, "I was nothing and would never be nothing." He would add salt to the wound with, "I could not make it without him, and no one would want me but him." He was in the military and would travel two weeks out of every year. Every year he would promise to take me but didn't. After he retired from the military 20 years later, we finally went away for the weekend. He was cold and distant. When we arrived he had conversations with others that were around, pretending he was this nice person, but did not want to be around, much less have a conversation with his own wife. But this was nothing new, so why did I think or hope one weekend away would change things.

The last night he went to the gift shop to purchase something. While he was gone I prepared the room and myself for romance; candle, rose petals, soft music; the works. What a fool I was, desperately trying to rekindle the sparks, the love, the tenderness. An hour later he returned with a bag from the gift shop that he slipped down between the dresser and the wall. It was for someone other than me. He proceeded to get in bed as if all I had done didn't exist. For a moment I thought, boy he should be thankful the old me (the one who would cut, fight or try to push him down the stairs) was gone, because I would be returning home alone. The fact was he did know that and that's why he did what he did.

Every now and then we have to put away the anger and hurt feelings aside and do the unexpected. What I should have done was, after fifteen minutes, got in the car and left him there. When we show vulnerability to those who don't care it opens us up to be hurt and walked on. We too often give them power to play us like puppets on a string. When we learn to channel the neglect, rejection and anger into positive constructive energy, then we can flip the script. Flipping the script does not mean get even because vengeance belongs to the Lord. However, it does mean that we acquire the power to change our life and not be susceptible to the things that trap us and keep us in bondage.

On the way back I asked him why he treated me so cold, as if I wasn't there or mattered, and he said that *"he loved me but he wasn't in love with me."* My entire world was destroyed again, my hope was gone. To say the least, the silence was empty and dark. I couldn't wait to get where I felt safe. Somehow between there and home I had to figure how to put on that "I'm okay face". What I really wanted to do was to hurt him like he hurt me. There was no reasoning or talking with him because, after he said what he had to say he just shut me out.

When he was upset he would repeat the same thing over and over until he got tired of hearing himself repeat it or I walked out the room. But when I asked him something or tried to hold a conversation he would look straight ahead as if I had said nothing. At first it would upset me. Then I calmed down only to get upset all over again. I had to work through it, but I hurt so bad. I loved him; how could he just destroy me like that? I cried and prayed and prayed and cried until God shut me up and made me listen to all the stuff I would tell others who were hurting. I have always hated to hear my own tape recordings because it was good food from God. So I listened, I wrote in my journal - Dump Book - until I released all of the hurt and pain. (*How to Journal Appendix 6*) I received sound counsel which helped me work through my stuff. It was then I realized I had stuff too. I couldn't put it all on him, so I faced me and dealt with me. It was during my makeover that I realized how important I was to me and to God. I had lost who I was and through this experience I uncovered me. Afterwards, I come to tell you that there is always an afterwards when we want change. Change is hard but necessary. When we cut ourselves healing and restoration only takes place after we have first cleaned the wound. We have to stop long enough to examine the problem, cut it into sections. Separate our stuff from others. Again ask the hard questions. If we need help, our pride has to be thrown out the window; get some professional help. The wound has to be cleaned of all the madness, the stuff, the garbage, the anger, rejection, etc. Second, the wound has to get some type of antiseptic in order to destroy the bacteria. The antiseptic is the Word of God, sound counsel, prayer or words of wisdom. Third, healing starts from the inside out, therefore we have to cover the wound until it heals. We have to get in a safe place and stay long enough for healing and restoration. That safe place could be a church, exercise class, NA or AA meetings, a support group, or just sitting by the water until you find your way.

Afterwards, I could turn my focus on what I needed to do in the relationship. I had grown to the point where his stupidity and arrogant behavior was on him and he had to take the responsibility for his own actions. I refused to take on his behavior, so I learned to answer my own questions and move on, because he wasn't worth the energy of getting angry, arguing and fighting. I learned how to give him to God and allow God to heal all my deep wounds. God began to create and develop in me the desire, abilities and capabilities of becoming a good counselor. I had the compassion to listen, not judge, but give guidance that was valued as life saving.

The other very important thing I learned was, if you really want to get even just love them in spite of their behavior. It takes less energy and thought to love than it does to be hateful and vindictive. It throws them off guard, they can't figure out why you are being not just nice but loving, and it kills them when they can't continue to dominate you. It took me a long time to learn that and it saved my life. I had to reach back into my memory bank and ask God why I was so restrained.

I was never a person to argue but if you push me in a corner I came out fighting. I learned I had a mean side that would fight to kill; I learned from my daddy; from having to protect my brother who had too much mouth and no backup until later when he grew taller and bigger; and from having to defend myself the year the schools were segregated. But fighting wasn't in my nature, until pushed.

We give and give much too much in all the wrong areas of our lives and there nothings left for anyone, including ourselves. When all of our energy and joy for the things that really matter have escaped us in the passing of time, we are left with the guilt and the shame of what we have lost and what we have become.

Many couples between work, home and other activities never take the time to listen, care or touch each other. They become wax cold, like two ships passing in the night, only blinking the light to avoid bumping into each other. You desire a kiss, a wink, or maybe a love tap on the back side; something, anything that would give you some hope that the flame hasn't gone all the way out. Instead you get a reminder of your responsibilities or things you have forgotten to do. Fear of being abused physically, sexually or emotionally, keeps you from asking, and seeking the necessary attention of your spouse. On prior occasions, when asked, you were accused of being callous and demanding. You're called everything but a child of God. He claims you don't understand that he's carrying too heavy a load to take on your insecurities. What happened to the open lines of communication, and the time when it wasn't one person who carried the load but it became a joint effort? Is it really a load or is it an excuse to shut you out or make you a punching bag, their sex doll, or raping you whenever they want sex, morning, noon and twice at night, riding you like a wild cowboy. No matter what you do it's never good enough.

As an alternative of being rejected, pushed, hit, or beaten again you crawl back into that dark place and close out the world. There are three indicators that are evidence of unresolved issues or guilt: 1. Defensive thinking mechanism – it's a distorted way of avoiding or reducing the feelings of anxiety, frustration and stress, 2. Condemnation – produced by inadequacy, weakness, low self-esteem, pessimism and insecurity, 3. Physical reaction

– physical tensions that are released through bodily action are distractions from emotional pain or guilt. These signs don't always reveal themselves until the victims of abuse inflict the same pain onto others or themselves when feeling guilty that we have stayed in an abusive situation too long or feel that there is no way out. Guilt has a way of motivating you to continue to use whatever device necessary to suppress the feelings and ultimately keep you in bondage. This process is called denial.

Denial is as deadly a killer as cancer, it slowly creeps in and takes over our lives. Everyone else sees the symptoms except the person in denial. Denial is defined as a problem that is not recognized or admitted as a problem irrespective of the extreme consequences. Denial comes in various forms:

1. *Rationalization* – having excuses or good reasons for everything that is done.

2. *Projection* – blaming others for your mistakes.

3. *Suppression* – consciously pushing away painful feelings and experiences out of the mind.

4. *Repression* – unconsciously removing from the mind painful thoughts, feelings and actions.

5. *Withdrawal* – purposely avoiding anything or anyone that brings about pain or discomfort.

The only way to defeat this behavior is to immediately accept where you are and what is necessary to break the cycle. Let's be clear, coming to grips with the pain is the first step in the process. This time you cannot mask the pain. Remove the pills, alcohol, drug, sex, people, things that you relied on to make you feel good, out of your path. Secondly, man/woman up and face that, "I'm a mess but I don't have to stay this way." Third, get some professional help. There is as much free help as there is costly help, and if you really want help you will pay the price even if you have to beg, borrow or steal, just like you did to stay in bondage.

I was there and had been there many times, you know, the point of no return; I wasn't going to take another rejection. I wasn't going to be left out, left behind or left alone another day. I wasn't going to take any more emotional abuse. His control over who I was and what I do for me was over. I was going to take back the control of my life. I needed a new perspective, a new lease on life; the old way of doing things had to go. This time I was ready, I had done my research, made the plan and worked the plan. I was through with being mad; I was armed and dangerous, pressed with the rest, to be blessed by the BEST.

Now let me tell you how I reached this major turning point in my life. I had to take a good long look at my life and realized that I had masked my hurt too long. We have to stop the rationalization and hear what others have said to help us. We must ask these hard questions:

- Is it true, am I in denial?

- Am I a victim of my own circumstances and, if, so what are they, and how am I a victim?

- Do I want to be free or continue in pain?

- How does freedom look? If you have been in bondage a long time you may not know what it looks like.

- Can I continue going in the same direction? If you are being physically abused your end could mean death, yours or someone else's?

- Am I sick and tired of being sick and tired of being right here, dangling on a puppet string? If so,

- How and where do I start when I have no money, job or job skills adequate to care for my kids and myself?

- Who is my support system?

- Where do I get help without him knowing?

- What resources do I have in my community and how do I get involved?

The next step for me was to be reconnected to God. In doing so, I learned that the way I viewed God was the way I viewed my father, and my husband who was suppose to be my protector; the one who would never abuse me or forsake me. I reached out to him but I didn't give him my whole heart, mind or soul. The walls were up; after all, I was angry with

God too. How could God let me marry this man? I was such an angry person. Once I reconnected with God and he forgave me, I was able to forgive others completely. Complete forgiveness comes when we give it all to God to handle and we get out of the way; then we can move on with our lives.

One church I attended preached all fire and brimstones, everything I wanted to do to have fun, I was told I would go to hell. Another church had the "name it, claim it" $$$$ lines; all I had was one dollar. I could feel the Elders Board looking down at me because of what I didn't have, as they came by and dropped a white cloth over my lap and rolled their eyes. Once I asked to speak to the Pastor. I had to go through the secretary, the security team, and another woman who drilled me like I wanted to have an affair with the Pastor. The bottom line was because I wasn't a member or part of the elite the answer, in no uncertain terms, was NO!!! They made me feel inadequate. I had been in bondage long enough and I was going to be in bondage in church too.

I wanted out of the marriage, but the church taught that God would send me to hell if I got a divorce. The only reason for divorce was adultery and then you could never remarry. Well I enjoyed the benefit of marriage security and sex. I exchanged security for bondage, and marital sex meant I wouldn't burn in hell. I stopped going to that church again for a short while. What I was unprepared for was the Lord had begun to change my heart, so I couldn't stay away from his Word. After a few months I visited a few other churches and the Lord led me to a church that really blessed me and changed my life. This time I had to go, because my marriage was crazy and I was losing it. Either I get some help or....... Have you ever been in an *"or place"*?

For the first time in my Christian walk I learned who Jesus was and who I was in Him. Wow, what a life changing experience. You see, you can't make this change by yourself, it requires the help of the master designer. God is the one who made us and not we ourselves. He has the blueprint for our lives. Everything that has happened between birth and death, good, bad or indifferent is part of the plan. In the end there is a purpose. God even knows when, how and why we step outside of His will, although He allows it to happen, because he gives us free will to choose. He has a plan to reconnect us to Him. What we don't understand is the consequences of stepping outside of His will. Though the consequences or the spanking can be severe, the blessing of restoration is far better. I truly thank Him for His grace and mercy.

It was the joy of receiving the abundant love from Jesus. You see, I couldn't love until I first received His love. This time I had to be willing to put down the fear and anger so Jesus could open my heart and heal the wounds that were so deep; I couldn't do that myself. I was looking for love and acceptance in all the wrong places. It isn't in people, sex, drugs, alcohol or things. You can try to please people all day long and still come up short.

The next important step; it was imperative for me to forgive. I have learned how to forgive with words but not from the heart. We say "I'm sorry," but what does that mean when we turn around and do the same thing repetitively. It means nothing to us or the recipient. There isn't anything about that forgiveness that makes sense. True forgiveness comes from the heart; therefore, you first have to have a spiritual heart transplant. If not, you'll think it is irrational and pointless to forgive someone who has hurt you, and will again if given the opportunity. However, God commands us to forgive unconditionally, no holding on to any fragments, completely letting go of the who, what, when and why. Yes, that's what forgiving and forgetting means. We have to be willing to tear up the little black book of every deed that was done. You truly have to be born again for this to give you a sense of peace. God's word says, *"For if you forgive men when they sin against you, your heavenly Father will also forgive you. But if you do not forgive men their sins, your Father will not forgive your sins,"* (Matt. 6:14-15). God died that my sins might be forgiven completely, and restored me completely, never to remember what wrong was done. He forgave, knowing I would repeat the wrong doings again. He will never bring it up again or keep record. On the other hand, we don't forgive or forget because we feel that we have to remember so we won't get hurt again.

Once I learned the freedom that forgiveness allowed me to have, it was on. I took back the final piece of control I gave away. There is so much power in those three words, "I forgive you" or "please forgive me." My husband would really push and I would go there with him, but after I realized what happened, I would stop and say to him, "Please forgive me for my behavior," and then leave the room or just stop talking. He once said angrily, how dare I forgive him, stop arguing, deem it to be over and leave him in his moment. I told him life was too precious to hold on to stuff that would eventually destroy me, and I was most valuable to me.

We can take back the control and gain the authority that God has given us to be free. The Word is clear in Galatians 5:1-3 (Message Bible),[1] *Christ has set us free to live a free life. So take your stand! Never again let anyone put a harness of slavery on you.* [2-3]*I am emphatic about this. The moment any one of you submits to circumcision or any other rule-keeping system, at that same moment Christ's hard-won gift of freedom is squandered. I repeat my warning: The person who accepts the ways of circumcision trades all the advantages of the free life in Christ for the obligations of the slave life of the law.*

CHAPTER 7

THE MASK HAS BEEN REMOVED BEGINS

The masks are so beautiful but yet so ugly, so foul, so distasteful; how could we possibly wear them for so long? Yes, they were at one time beautiful, however, after all of our pain, hurts, disappointments, rejection, abuse, and all our open wounds that were hiding behind the mask began to seep out, the mask became indecent.

During Women's Ministry, many times I'll use as an illustration (to show how indecent the stuff is that we hide in and on us) how as young girls before tampons we wore napkins. These napkins had to be changed often, however, some were too embarrassed to change them in public places in fear of being identified. They would wear them all day. Now let your mind think back, if you can, to how nasty that would look and smell. Hold on to that picture and add three or four weeks worth of continuous discharge all on the same napkin; now visualize it..... place it in front of you..... that represents the macabre (*related to or like the "dance of death", in which death, as a skeleton, leads other skeletons to the grave*) mask, which is your mask, and the skeletons lead you to your grave.

We don't see how demoralizing and deadly it is, we only know the fear that keeps it on. Instead, we must convert the fear that cripples to fear that provokes, until we are completely unmasked. The first reaction to what you see is to replace the mask. We ask ourselves if others see and smell what we see and smell. We vacillate for a moment; the fear of destruction outweighs the demand to remain hidden. We are now faced with the compelling decision to change. Change isn't something we want, accept easily, or know how to do, but understand we must change. We don't know how we got here so we have to assume that it was by a power greater than us, therefore, it has to be a power greater than us working on the inside to perfect us on the outside. Psalm 135:5 (NIV) says, *"I know that the LORD is great, that our Lord is greater than all gods."*

"Ye are of God, little children, and have overcome them: because greater is he that is in you, than

he that is in the world." 1 John 4:4 (KJ) Once we acknowledge we want help, release our will which prevents us from moving forward, and accept the will and path of the Creator, he begins this mighty transformation in our lives.

We try to comprehend and understand the mysteries of the why's and the how's of our messed up, unmanageable, problematic, and devastated life. Therefore, we must have the Creator who designed us leading, guiding and calibrating the way through our wrong turns and choices in life; which is the reason He tells us to *"Trust in the LORD with all your heart and lean not on our own understanding; in all your ways acknowledge him, and he will make your paths straight."* Proverbs 3:5-7 (NIV)

Because of the devastation we can't move, turn, remove or destroy the mask, and not return to the same devastating situation without God's help. It is unquestionable that we must take ownership of the condition under the mask, however, God has created the mask to protect us until we are ready for it to be removed. If in fact God created the mask, he is the only one that knows how to remove it layer by layer at the precise time, with accurate and precise reconstruction. Not allowing us to hold on to painful situations, people and things because it's safer to keep the familiar than risk the hard task of change. We don't know how to change, why we should change, or what to change into. If a caterpillar knew that he would have to crawl up a tree, build a cocoon for himself, and then go through a painful transformation he would stop the process before it started. It has to journey the path to become a beautiful bufferfly. God too, wants to transform us into beautiful butterflies, but we fight so hard not to be lead into the cocoons. But we go so willingly into the wrong direction.

Getting free was a long process for me. The more I learned about me the more I wanted to turn back. One thing I learned at the end of each road was if I stayed on the path to the end through all of the road blocks, struggles, trials and temptations, in conclusion I was a better, stronger person. It was like peeling an onion, it was painful but necessary. Each layer has its own deficiencies we must rid ourselves of. Let's look at the layers.

There are four things to know in order to begin the process out of bondage: (1) we first have to be sick and tired of being sick and tired of being in the situation we are in; identify where we are, who and what we have become; who and what has us bound. The first layer is denial and false perceptions. This layer is the protector of all the hurt, wounds and self-infliction. When we pull this layer off we have to be ready to face depression, rejection, and abandonment. You have to face the real truth, no more excuses, no more hiding, controlling, or being controlled. The truth hurts when you can't blame anyone anymore. We are where we are because we made a decision to be here, and now we have to make a decision to change. (2) Admit we can't get out on our own, we need a power greater than our own, we need God the Creator to create a way out. Allow God to do whatever's necessary to transform us into beautiful creations. Whether you have to close yourself in a cocoon or pull the layer off yourself like an onion, just demand and decree a change. Yes, shed the tears, scream, holler; but get up, dust yourself off, ask for forgiveness and get ready for the next step. (3) This is the second hardest. After we learn the truth about us and we step into the change process, we have to now take ownership of all the bad, ugly behaviors that are tangled like weeds in the good grass. The change process requires that we pull the weeds. It's finding out that you were too high maintenance, too controlling, too bossy, too shy, too timid, too lonely, too needy, too co-dependent, too enabling, too jealous, too overbearing, and too...... Eliminating the root of the behavior was part of the first and second step, but know you are faced with the behaviors and they are harder to change. Alcoholics are often called dry drunks because they have stopped drinking, but the behavior has not changed. The behavior has to change also; it's attached to the same messy root problem. Decide to be made whole, not patched up. Give everything to the Lord, he knows us better than we know ourselves. Sit down and write down all the bad behaviors and replace them with good behaviors so they don't return. Water them with the Word of God, fertilize with praise and worship, weed by fasting and praying, and reseed by being a doer of His Word in the areas of weakness. (4)The old you will be gone and behold it's the new you. Except the new you, embrace the new you, learn and love the new you, and know that you were created with an absolute, unconditional, supreme purpose. So peel off the last onion skin or step out the cocoon, fly and never turn back again.

The only purpose of the enemy is to keep us from reaching our unmovable, unchangeable God given destiny. So he distracts us with all kinds of things or people; attempts to destroy us emotionally, financially, physically and spiritually; he attacks our character, who we are, where we come from and where we are going; he then tells us we have no purpose, and without a purpose there is no hope. Oh, but I come to tell you today that God has an absolute purpose for each of our lives and that purpose is unconditional. It is and always will be ours to obtain. It's supreme because God loves us so much that his gifts are rich in abundance.

His first gift to us is His Son, Jesus Christ, who shed His blood for us for the remission of our sins (that's the "being sick and tired" and "I need Jesus--my way out" salvation). Second, sanctification - the blood that we can't see, feel or taste; the blood that we have to have working faith in order to see that it has washed us clean, white as snow, purified us of every unclean thing that has touched, filled, changed, or hurt us; every dirty thing that we have touched or allowed into our minds and heart; and everything wrong that we have thought or done. Third, He justified us – oh, now don't think that you have arrived on your own, we have the rich gifts of the gracious and merciful God, not because of anything we have done. No, we didn't and still don't deserve most of what He has given us. *"And we have such trust through Christ toward God. Not that we are sufficient of ourselves to think of anything as being from ourselves, but our sufficiency is from God, who also made us sufficient."* 2 Corinthians 3:4-6 (NKJ)

CHAPTER 8

I'M FREE
NO MORE CHAINS HOLDING
ME

I'm free, praise the LORD I'm free, no longer bound, no more chains holding me; my soul is resting, it's just a blessing, praise the Lord, hallelujah I'm free. The song writer must have been thinking of me when that was written. I am free and I have to praise the Lord, because it is because of him that I am free.

I had to clean house; there was no one to lean on: no husband, kids, friends, job, car, and even some of the furniture was gone. While the Lord had me prostrate before him, I reflected back to one Sunday I was preaching, and the Lord said he was going to remove all the hindrances in my life. All the hindrances were gone -- **"I was free"**. I felt the burdens lift and shackles come off. I was new, brand spanking new. I went to the movies, walks, and dinner alone, yet not alone. The Lord became my husband. We had a relationship that was so sweet. He courted me, held me, kissed me, and most of all LOVED ME for me until I could love me for me.

My daughters and close friends had said that I had resilience and no matter what came my way I always bounced back. This time, this season I did bounce back, I soared forward.

In closing, I leave the following testimony with you. There once was a lady who was caught in a bad situation. It was her accusers who had been intimate with her that brought her to Jesus to be stoned. Jesus suggested that they who were without sin could cast the first stone. When he lifted His head He asked her, "Where are your accusers?" This lady would say to you today, "Take it to the Lord and you will find that he will release you from the bondage of your accusers." (John 8:4-8)

Another woman said, "I was put out of town because I had a twelve year issue. But one day I heard that Jesus was coming through town and I made a decision that enough was enough. I had to get past the gatekeeper, but I couldn't get through in my present mind set. I had tried everybody who was somebody and received no help; I had nothing to lose except my issue." She knew three things: this man named Jesus was her solution; she had faith that she would be healed, and lastly, she knew that she would never return to that place in her life. She got up and cleaned up, did her hair, nails, toes, put on some makeup and her best outfit. Her faith, which she stood up in, allowed her to be changed then, she was new then, and when she reached the gatekeeper he did not recognized her nor stop her. She would say, "I didn't stop there, I humbled myself, fell to my knees and crawled until I reached Jesus' hem and I touched him. I didn't need Him to touch me, I believed that there was enough power in him to make me whole. I could have gone home once I entered the gate, but just being healed wasn't enough, so do what you have never done before to get what you have never received, and be made whole." Jesus turned and asked, "Who touched me?" When she replied, Jesus told the woman, "Your faith has made you whole." (Mark 5:25-34) Get up right where you are in your mess, make a decision to change, dust yourself off, take the first step and Jesus will meet you and take you the rest of the way.

Now there are times when only Jesus will tell you to do something that is totally ridiculous, crazy or even foolish. However, if we have been a fool for the devil what do we have to lose?

There was a man with leprosy named Naaman who was told by God through the prophet Elisha to, "Wash in the Jordon seven times and your flesh will be restored and you will be made clean." Naaman thought like we would: this has to be the dumbest thing I've ever heard of. Why would he, who was infected, wash in dirty water, not one time but seven times, and risk becoming more infected? He returned home angry because he had to travel all the way back to the Jordon River to do what God had told him to do first. I ask, how much faith does it take to move beyond your faith perimeter? Do you have enough faith to match the answer or solution that we need to be made whole? Naaman, I believe, had to wash in dirty water, had he washed in clean water he would have contaminated the clean water. You have to leave dirt in dirt. But why seven times? Seven represents complete. I believed that, like us, the first six times he washed and complained, but on the seventh time something happened on the inside, and this time he began to praise God from whom all blessings flow. Praise him for who God was, is and will be; praise him just because. I believe the last time he forgot why he was washing, forgot to look to see if he had changed, forgot himself and focused on the matchless God. And because he washed this seventh time in obedience and gratitude of being in the presence of God, he was restored and cleansed. He forgot about himself and concentrated on God, not for what he wanted but for who He was.

God can and is willing to make you whole. We have to be willing to give everything to Him. And when we do, He will destroy every chain, shackle, everything, and everyone including self, that holds us captive. God's plan is for no more chains to hold you. What about you? Do you want to be free? Paul writes in Galatians 5:1, *"Stand fast therefore in the liberty by which Christ has made us free, and do not be entangled again with a yoke of bondage."*

PRAYER OF SALVATION

BY: PASTOR L. ALPHONSO DENT

Father, I come by faith, to you in the matchless name of Jesus. Believing in your Word that you desire all men to be saved and come into the knowledge of the truth.

Father, I bring _____ before you this day, asking for his/her forgiveness of all sins and blot out his/her transgressions committed against you and others.

Father, I take authority over Satan and every demonic spirit sent with an assignment to restrain and prohibit him/her from accepting you as Lord and Savior.

Father, I cry unto you that _____ will open his/her heart and eyes and come to the realization that you sent your son Jesus Christ to die and rose again for him/her; repent by confessing his/her sins, believing in their heart, trust and rely on you as Lord.

Father, please come in to his/her life and extend your love, mercy and soul saving grace.

Father, if you stopped Saul on the road of Damascus, save and changed his life I know surely you can save my _____ _____.

Please break the power and hold that Satan has over his/her life and loosen the powerful and active Gospel into his/her hearing and understanding.

Oh Lord my God, I now give _____ unto you and leave him/her in your mighty and capable hands believing that all things work together and are fitting into your plan for your good pleasure.

I thank you, in Jesus Name, Amen.

PRAYER OF DELIVERANCE FOR MARRIAGE

BY: STEPHANIE BLANKS, Ph.D.

Father, I thank you for being in the midst of our marriage and we ask that you will continue to bless us and lead us.

Father, I thank you for being the light in the midst of times of darkness and being the peace in the midst of struggles.

I thank you for being a source of strength in the times of our weakness and a comforter in the times of sorrows.

Father, I ask that you protect us against the works of the enemy and the works of our flesh. Cover us in wisdom and understanding.

Let us walk in love, trust and patience.

Father, I pray during difficult times we will stand together; we will be sensitive, respectful and gentle towards each other's feelings and position.

I come against any attempts of the enemy to kill, steal or destroy what you have put together.

We bind the spirit of jealousy, malice and revenge when one of our feelings has been hurt. I pray for forgiveness to be abundant and long suffering to be fruitful in our marriage.

Father, we ask that our love will continue to grow and our hearts will continue to be filled with joy and peace.

Wife prays for her husband:

Father, I pray that you bless my husband.

Please give Him wisdom to navigate through the uncertainties of the day and open his awareness to the tricks and tactics of the enemy.

Father, I pray that you will deliver him from the smears and plots that the enemy has set for him because no weapon formed against him will prosper.

Deliver him from any childhood hurts, disappointments and soul ties that will cause him to be doubtful about who you are and the plans you have for him.

Father, I pray that he will walk according to your word and your ways. I pray that he will live for you and serve you with all his heart.

I decree and declare that he is a blessed man and knowledgeable of your ways.

He is the head and not the tail.

He is a wise man one who is proficient in providing for his family; he finds favor in whatever he puts his hands too.

He is skilled in his business affairs and compassionate in his Kingdom relationship.

Father, I thank you that my husband finds peace in my arms and love in my heart; he sees hope in my eyes and joy in my smile.

I thank you Father in Jesus Name Amen.

Husband prays for his wife:

Father, I thank you for giving my wife to me as my gift for she is bone of my bone and flesh of my flesh. We are one and we stand unified against the tricks of the enemy.

Father, I pray that strength and wisdom will cover her and truth will lead her.

Father, I pray against issues generational curses and the pain of her past.

I pray against low self esteem, personal doubt and feeling of mistrust.

I decree and declare that she is a virtuous woman who is blessed coming in and going out.

Whatever she puts her mind and hands to will bring forth great success in her business affairs as well as her covenant relationships.

I pray that she will prosper and be in good health even as her soul prospers.

I thank you, in Jesus' Name, Amen

PRAYER OF DELIVERANCE FOR LOW SELF-ESTEEM AND LONELINESS

BY: EVANGLIST KIMBERELY THOMAS

Father, I come to you in the Matchless name of Jesus.

I ask in your name Jesus, that you would deliver me from the spirit of loneliness that causes me to feel isolated, alone, rejected, wounded and unloved.

Deliver me from the spirit of solitarily standing apart from others in isolation.

I bind the spirit of loneliness and all its attachments, low-esteem, lack of confidence, lack of assurance, lack of possession. I bind the lack of ability to love self and all of its attachments.

I command you Satan, to leave in the name of Jesus. I command that you go to the outer darkness and never to return.

I loosen the spirit of self love, friendship, and freedom to know others.

I loosen the spirit of self acceptance and the spirit of love for myself.

I loosen the spirit of self confidence, assurance self possession belief in my ability and trust in Jesus Name.

I thank you Lord that the spirit of loneliness is gone and I am free in Jesus Name.

PRAYER OF DELIVERANCE FOR REJECTION BASED ON GENESIS 3:6-13

BY: EVANGLIST KIMBERELY THOMAS

Father, I come to you in the Name of Jesus and I bind the strongman called the spirit of rejection.

I bind the spirit of rejection in the Name of Jesus along with all of Satan's works, roots, fruits, tentacles, links and the other ungodly spirits that are in my life.

I come against the spirits of:

Rejection by others

Rejection of others

Self rejection and

Rejection of God

I cast you out of me in Jesus Name.

Satan I command you to release the hold you have on me and I cast you out of me along with all of your works, roots, fruit, tentacles, links, and spirits.,

I now cast you into outer darkness in the name of Jesus.

I command you to not come back into my presence again.

I ask you heavenly Father in the Name of Jesus

to loosen today the spirit of adoption, acceptance, and your everlasting love into my spirit according to Romans 8:15.

I thank you Lord for setting me free in Jesus Name, Amen.

PRAYER OF DELIVERANCE

BY: DR. FRANCINE DENT

Father, I thank you for being in my life as my Lord and Savior.

I thank you, because I have a personal relationship with you and I understand that except a man is born again he cannot see the kingdom of God.

I clearly remember when I used to say there is no God, what a fool I was.

It was a peace that came in the midst of the storm in my life that allowed me to see you as a merciful, loving and real God.

Thank you for saving me. I need you now to come In and change my heart, my mind and my lifestyle.

Father, I thank you because I now understand that I am blessed, I am fearfully and wonderfully made and because of your forgiveness and love for me I ask for forgiveness for all the hurtful things I have done.

Please forgive me for allowing separation, division, strife, anger, bitterness, and jealousy,

to play a destructive role in my life.

Father, forgive me for allowing my children, relatives, and others be my lord. I had a need to control them by making them feel unimportant and unwanted which results in rejection and neglect.

Father, I come against all substance abuse, verbal assassination, physical, emotional abuse; every lie, selfish and vain thing that I have thought or done. I come against the spirit of manipulation, soul ties; learned behaviors, generational curses, mental health, territorial demise, and self destructive behaviors.

I pray the hand of the enemy and weapons that I thought, shaped or formed against others will not prosper.

Father, I thank you for totally and completely forgiving me and restoring me again.

Father, I speak light into every situation and life into every dead thing.

I pray that when in turmoil and confusion the result will be peace.

Father, I declare that I will love you from the depth of my heart. I desire that my love for you will grow, thirsty like a deer that pants for water.

Father, I decree that each need be met and that you feed me until I am abundantly satisfied in you and you alone.

Father, I decree that your word be hid in my heart causing me to not sin against you again. Let your mercy and grace fall; heal, restore, establish, stabilize, seal and anoint past and new relationships.

Let me always walk in the path of righteousness, being the evidence of a Godly covenant that flourishes the fruits of your Spirit.

In the name of Jesus, Amen

WHO AM I

WORKBOOK – EXERCISE 1

WHO AM I

NAME:_____

DATE OF BIRTH:_____ AGE:_____

YOUR PARENTS: (CIRCLE L for living or D for decrease)

    MOTHER_____ L D

    FATHER _____ L D

    OTHER _____ _____ L D

    _____ _____ L D

OTHER PERSONS OF INFLUENCE IN YOUR LIFE AS A CHILD:

NAME:_____ RELATION:_____

NAME:_____ RELATION:_____

NAME:_____ RELATION:_____

NAME:_____ RELATION:_____

WHERE DID YOU LIVE: _____

WHERE DID YOU GO TO SCHOOL

    ELEMENTARY:_____

    MIDDLE: _____

    HIGH: _____

    COLLEGE: _____

WHO AM I
PAGE 2

*HOW DID THEY INFLUENCE YOU AND WAS THE
EXPERIENCE GOOD, NOT GOOD BUT HELPFUL
LATER IN LIFE, OR DETRIMENTAL?*

WHO AM I
PAGE 3

LIST YOUR JOYFUL EXPERIENCES AND YOUR PAINFUL/HURT ONES:

PAINFUL/HURT EXPERIENCES

JOYFUL/HAPPY EXPERIENCES

WHO AM I
PAGE 4

HOW DID THEY INFLUENCE YOUR LIFE NEGATIVELY OR POSITIVELY? USE THE EXPERIENCE IN THE PREVIOUS CHART.				
JOYFUL/HAPPY EXPERIENCE	POS. ✓	NEG ✓	HOW	WHY

WHO AM I
PAGE 5

REVIEW ALL THE INFORMATION AND ASK YOURSELF WHO, WHAT AND HOW HAVE YOU ALLOWED THOSE INFLUENCES TO AFFFECT YOUR LIFE AND WHAT ARE YOU GOING TO DO ABOUT IT NOW?

WRONG TURNS/ WRONG DECISIONS

WORKSHEET – EXERCISE 2

(1) What did you do, How it happen or how often, When or where the behavior occurred, and why did I make the wrong turns/wrong decision,

(2) What do you need to stop the behavior,

(3) What new behavior do you need to start immediately?

(4) Make a plan to be victorious. Be specific (answer when, how long and what you are to do)

_____

_____

_____

_____

_____

Matthew 7:1,5 1 "Do not judge, or you too will be judged 5 You hypocrite, first take the plank out of your own eye, and then you will see clearly to remove the speck from your brother's eye.

WORKSHEET – EXERCISE 3

LEARN YOUR PERSONALITY PROFILE

D I S C

WWW.UNIQUELYYOU.COM

TAKE THE PERSONALITY TEST BY LINKING TO THIS WEBSITE TO LEARN WHAT YOUR DISC IS AND LEARN MORE ABOUT WHO YOU ARE. FIND OUT WHERE THE NEXT SEMINARS ARE GIVEN

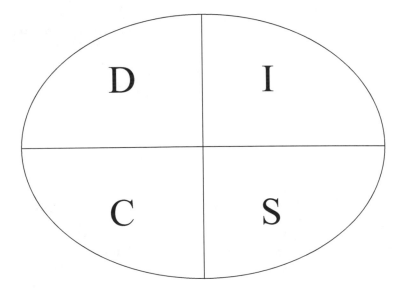

DISC TYPES

We are composites of all four types, but we tend to be more of one or two than the other. It is common to have two stronger traits, while being not as motivated by the others. Each type stands alone with its own recognizable characteristic.

"D" TYPES

"D" types are more direct, demanding, decisive, and dominant. As active / task-oriented individuals they are determined to get the job done. They are very industrious and forceful. They are strong leaders who like to be bosses.

On the down side "D" can be too domineering and demanding. They tend to be impatient and insensitive. They love challenges and strive hard to succeed in accomplishing tasks. "D" needs to guard against the overuse of their strengths.

"I" TYPES

Influencing and inspiring types are "I"s. They are more exciting and enthusiastic. They love the crowd, the more the merrier. As great communicators, they love to talk. They tend to outshine everyone. Popularity is important to them.

Ego and self-centeredness are their weaknesses. They tend to seek the lime-light. They desire lots of attention and praise. Often upfront and more outgoing than all the other types, they can "steal the show." Humility and quietness are their greatest challenges.

"S" TYPES

These are the most submissive, sensitive, and soft types. They tend to be more reserved than the others. Their loyal and sweet spirits makes them everyone's friends. They often volunteer, not to be seen or recognized, but to simply help others.

People often take advantage of their kindness. They are vulnerable to manipulation and intimidation. Their desire to please makes them seem like weak individuals. They need to speak out and take charge. Ironically, they can be extremely protective when people threaten their loved ones' security.

"C" TYPES

When you think of the competent, cautious, calculating, careful, and critical thinking types, you are describing "C" types. It is not like them to be impulsive or to jump into things.

They prefer clear instructions. They are more compliant when it comes to right and wrong. "Going by the book" is one of their strongest motivations.

At the same time, they can be extremely moody and picky. Their concern for correctness often overshadows their care for what people think or feel. They tend to be "loners," disinterested in an exciting social life. Thinking things through often makes them slow decision makers and unbending types.

Each of the "D," "I," "S" and "C" types have their strengths and "uniqueness." The following link www. UniquelyYou.com will give you more information on each type and how you can have an extreme personality makeover to control your strengths and avoid their weaknesses. You can also take the personality test by going to www.UniquelyYou.net and then click on Extreme Personality Makeover.

Permission given by Mels Carbonell, Ph.D. author of Extreme Personality Makeover and So, You're Unique! What's your Point?

GRIEF

WORKSHEET – EXERCISE 4

UNDERSTANDING LOSS

THE FIVE STAGES OF GRIEF

1. DENIAL
   - Denial: when someone refuses to believe the reality of the situation

   - The person doesn't want to believe someone has died or has a terminal illness

2. ANGER
   - Anger is a normal feeling associated with loss.

   - People express their anger differently.

   - They may be mad at the person who is sick or who died or left them.

- They may be angry at someone they think caused the illness or loss.

- They may be angry at themselves believing that they are responsible for the illness or death or loss.

3. BARGAINING
   - Bargaining takes place when someone attempts to talk their way out of the illness or death.

   - They may say, "I promise I will be better if you get well or come back" or "I will get better grades and keep my room clean if you don't die."

4. DEPRESSION
   - Depression means that someone feels sadness and hurt because of the illness or death.

   - That person may cry excessively and withdraw by staying away from people.

- They may experience loss of appetite and/or sleep.

5. ACCEPTANCE
   - Acceptance indicates that someone understands that a certain person is no longer with them or is going to die and has come to terms with the situation.

WHAT THE BIBLE SAY ABOUT GRIEF

2 Samuel 12:15, 16, 21, 22, 23 NIV

¹⁵ After Nathan had gone home, the LORD struck the child that Uriah's wife had borne to David, and he became ill. ¹⁶ David pleaded with God for the child. He fasted and spent the nights lying in sackcloth on the ground. ²¹ His attendants asked him, "Why are you acting this way? While the child was alive, you fasted and wept, but now that the child is dead, you get up and eat!" ²² He answered, "While the child was still alive, I fasted and wept. I thought, 'Who knows? The LORD may be gracious to me and let the child live.' ²³ But now that he is dead, why should I go on fasting? Can I bring him back again? I will go to him, but he will not return to me."

1 Corinthians 10:13 NIV

¹³ No temptation has overtaken you except what is common to mankind. And God is faithful; he will not let you be tempted beyond what you can bear. But when you are tempted, he will also provide a way out so that you can endure it.

2 Corinthians 1:3 NIV

³ Praise be to the God and Father of our Lord Jesus Christ, the Father of compassion and the God of all comfort,

1 Thessalonians 4:13-17 NIV

¹³ Brothers and sisters, we do not want you to be uninformed about those who sleep in death, so that you do not grieve like the rest of mankind, who have no hope. ¹⁴ For we believe that Jesus died and rose again, and so we believe that God will bring with Jesus those who have fallen asleep in him. ¹⁵ According to the Lord's word, we tell you that we who are still alive, who are left until the coming of the Lord, will certainly not precede those who have fallen asleep. ¹⁶ For the Lord himself will come down from heaven, with a loud command, with the voice of the archangel and with the trumpet call of God, and the dead in Christ will rise first. ¹⁷ After that, we who are still alive and are left will be caught up together with them in the clouds to meet the Lord in the air. And so we will be with the Lord forever.

Romans 8:28 NIV

²⁸ And we know that in all things God works for the good of those who love him, who have been called according to his purpose.

OTHER SCRIPTURES FOR HOPE

Psalm 116:15

John 3:36; 10:28; 11:25, 26, 35, 36

Hebrews 4:15, 16

1 Peter 5:7

James 4:8

MY ANXIETY LOG
WORKSHEET – EXERCISE 5

WRITE THE SPECIFIC PROBLEM	WHEN IT HAPPENS		HOW OFTEN						
What happened; How did it make you feel; What did you do; Are others involved?	Place	Time	S	M	T	W	T	F	S

ANXIETY PATTERN

EVALUATE BEHAVIOR THAT OCCURRED MORE THAN THREE TIMES. THEN COMPLETE WRONG TURNS.

1. What happened?_____

_____

_____

2. How did it make you feel? _____

_____

_____

3. What did you do?_____

_____

_____

4. Are others involved?_____

_____

_____

5. What behaviors do you need not to repeat?__

_____

_____

JOURNALING
KEEPING A DUMP BOOK

I like to call it a Dump Book. This is a process whereby you dump your feelings, frustrations, anxiety, anger and all other emotions in to a book. These emotions should never be inflicted on another person neither should they be held within. These suppressed emotions will erupt and eventually spill over. So journaling or dumping allows you to get those feelings out of you. Here are some helpful tips for dumping.

1. Purchase a spiral or composition notebook or make a dump book.

2. Find a hiding place that's out of reach of others.

3. Write, draw or both what you feel or need to say but can't.

4. Dump until you get it all out.

5. For some you may just need to write the name down and scratch or mark through it. As you do, say what you need to say to that person.

6. For me, I write at the top on my page, Dear Lord I place this that I write in your hands and out of my hands and heart. When I finish I say thank you for taking this which was too heavy for me.

7. Those words/conversations that are really hurtful may need to be removed, burned or torn up.

8. Don't be concerned about spelling or how you say what you write; garbage isn't pretty but necessary.

If you are having problems communicating with your spouse without arguing, try not talking verbally, for a week and writing your conversation. When you learn how to soften what you say and how you say it, with love, you can resume talking.

1. Stop talking and start listening to what you are saying.

2. Write what you would say, then read it to yourself and to hear what and how you have said it.

3. If it is not uplifting but tearing the other person down, rewrite it before giving it to the person.

4. You may need to dump before you give the other person your note.

5. It's ok to put some time between the notes. It's better to delay than to destroy.

6. Use spoken words only when necessary or you have to include others (kids, guest, etc.)

7. Never use a third party to say what you should write.

COPYRIGHT PERMISSIONS

UNIQUELY YOU HUMAN ROUSOURCES

MELS CARBONELL, Ph.D.

P.O. Box 490

Blue Ridge, GA 30513

To order:

DISC Personalities (Adults, Parents, Teens, & Child)

Professional/Leaders DISC Personality Profile

Discover Your Giftedness

Conference calls

Online Certification Training and more

(800) 501-0490, info. (706)492-5490

www.myuy.com or www.UniquelyYou.NET

OTHER SUGGESTED MATERIAL

CHURCH VIPERS

By: Rodney D. Stewart

A Book of Hope, A Book of Healing,

A Book of Exposure

www.trafford.com,

www.church-vipers.weebly.com

(800) 232-4444

LET IT GO

BY: Virginia Harrison, Ph.D.

This book is about the struggles one woman encountered in her life and the difficulties she had in letting those struggles go.

www.Xulonpress.com

www.amazon.com

Barnes & Noble

John 3 16 Christian Bookstore